AL-GHAZĀLĪ

Inner Dimensions of Islamic Worship

Translated from the *Iḥyā'* by
Muhtar Holland

THE ISLAMIC FOUNDATION

Published by
THE ISLAMIC FOUNDATION,
Markfield Conference Centre,
Ratby Lane, Markfield,
Leicestershire, LE67 9SY,
United Kingdom
Email: publications@islamic-foundation.com
Website: www.islamic-foundation.com

Quran House, Po Box 30611, Nairobi, Kenya

PMB 3196, Kano, Nigeria

Distributed by
Kube Publishing Ltd.
Tel: +44(0)1530 249230, Fax: +44(0)1530 249656
e-mail: info@kubepublishing.com

14th impression, 2023

British Library Cataloguing in Publication Data
Al-Ghazali : Inner dimensions of Islamic worship
1. Worship (Islam)
I. Title II. Ihya al-ulum al-din. English
297'.43 B1842

ISBN 978-0-86037-126-7 Casebound
ISBN 978-0-86037-125-0 Paperback

Printed by Elma Basim, Turkey

بسم الله الرحمن الرحيم

Contents

Intention – Takbīr – Opening Invocations –
Reciting the Quran – Bowing Down – Prostration –
Sitting and Testifying – End of Supplication –
Salutation

Stories of the Humble

Fine Points of Propriety; Internal Conduct

Purity of Intention and Means – Shunning Unlawful
Taxes – Moderation in Expenditure – Forsaking
Evil Conduct – Going on Foot – Modesty and

Simplicity of Transport – Shabbiness in Dress and
Appearance – Kindness to Beasts of Burden –
Sacrificing Animals – Equanimity

INNER STATES AT VARIOUS STAGES OF ḤAJJ

Understanding – Yearning – Resolve – Severing
Ties – Provisions – Transport – Purchase of *Iḥrām* –
Leaving Home – Crossing the Desert – Putting on
Iḥrām and Crying 'Labbayk' – Entering Makka –
Seeing the Ka'ba – Circumambulating the House
(*Ṭawāf*) – Touching the Black Stone – Standing
at Multazam – Running between al-Ṣafā and
al-Marwa (Sa'*y)* – Standing at 'Arafāt – Casting
Pebbles (*Ramy*) – Sacrificing Animals – Visiting
Madina – Visiting God's Messenger

Transliteration Table

Consonants. Arabic

initial: unexpressed medial and final:

ء	ʾ	د	d	ض	ḍ	ك	k
ب	b	ذ	dh	ط	ṭ	ل	l
ت	t	ر	r	ظ	ẓ	م	m
ث	th	ز	z	ع	ʿ	ن	n
ج	j	س	s	غ	gh	هـ	h
ح	ḥ	ش	sh	ف	f	و	w
خ	kh	ص	ṣ	ق	q	ي	y

Vowels, diphthongs, etc.

Short:	ـَ	a	ـِ	i	ـُ	u
long:	ـَا	ā	ـِي	ī	ـُو	ū
diphthongs:			ـَوْ	aw		
			ـَيْ	ay		

Foreword

'Except he who comes to God with a heart, pure and whole', says the Quran, no one shall receive the Inheritance of the Garden of Bliss, of the everlasting Life of happiness, near Allah, 'on the day when they are raised up, the day when neither riches nor children shall avail.' (al-Shu'arā', 26:85-9); the goal and the promise is not far, but only for him 'who turns often unto God and keeps Him always in heart; who fears, without seeing, the most Merciful, and comes with a penitent heart.' (Qāf, 50: 27-8) On the other hand, only those that 'in their hearts is disease' (al-Baqarah, 2:10) shall be denied this Inheritance; they have eyes which can see as far as the farthest galaxies and as deep as the heart of an atom, but they are unable to peep inside themselves for 'it is not the eyes that are blind, but blind are the hearts within the breasts.' (al-Ḥajj, 22: 46) Who shall, therefore, not care to nurture the life in the heart – his inner world – as he lives his life in the world, in responding to his God?

Life has many dimensions, many layers, many phases. On the one hand, all of them should exist fused together, in continuing dynamic interaction with each other. For life is an integrated whole. It would be folly to so atomise and analyse life as to end up looking at it as through a microscope – seeing only one *dimension* at a time, magnified disproportionately; or with a telescope, resulting in simplistic reductionism. To employ tunnel vision is to live with an unbalanced concern for one aspect and a disregard of others. In all ages men have committed this folly, but perhaps never on the same scale as today. The consequences of this disproportion and imbalance are disastrous: disintegration of person and society, as one lives in one dimension alone, or in disregard of the wholeness of life.

On the other hand, in concern for the wholeness of life, it would be unwise not to recognise each dimension separately and ensure that it has its proper place in the pursuits of life, is looked after and nurtured properly and plays its proportionate role in the development of a person. Only by guarding against both errors can one ensure freedom from anxiety and sorrow and happiness and prosperity, here and in the Hereafter.

Al-Ghazālī, in his characteristically powerful, penetrating and inspiring way, leads us in this book into the world of the inner dimensions of worship in Islam. Do not be misled by the title; such is the poverty of human language that we could not choose any better. Worship in Islam is not only observance of the prescribed worship rites – Prayer, Almsgiving, Fasting, Pilgrimage – but living one's entire life in obedience to God, doing His will and seeking His pleasure, exactly in the way He has laid down. But the worship rites are the essential, and the only, key to that full life of worship. And it is with their inner dimensions that this book is primarily concerned. Also, do not let the word 'inner' make us think that al-Ghazālī is embarking upon any venture to effect a split between the 'inner' and the 'outer', or is going to suggest any esoteric meanings behind the exoteric forms of worship as found in the *Sharī'ah.* He is not. His 'inner' dimensions include things like praying at the proper time, congregational Prayers, balance and proportion in the outward movements in Prayer, finding the right type of persons to give Alms to, journeying for Pilgrimage with legitimately earned money and caring for animals on the way, etc., etc.

Al-Ghazālī is a towering figure in Islam; his influence is enormous. He is also controversial; perhaps no great man can escape controversy. Many have written criticising him. Echoing some of their concerns, though very exaggeratedly, a former European Sufi, in examining the split of inward and outward, castigates al-Ghazālī thus: 'yet this split – between dhahir and batin – this license to make half-men - outward legalists *or* [emphasis mine] inward experience-ists – had come from al-Ghazali and his notorious *Ihya.* Indeed his reputation [that he 'brought together the Sufis and the legalists'] rests on the very opposite of his accomplishment . . . he surgically separated the body from its life support' (Shaykh Abdal Qadir al-Murabit, *Root Islamic Education,* Norwich, p.135). However, the dominant view is quite succinctly summarised by Annemarie Schimmel: 'All that Ghazālī teaches . . . is only to help man to live a life in accordance with the sacred law, not by clinging *exclusively* [emphasis mine] to its letter, but by an understanding of its deeper meaning, by sanctification of the whole life, so that he is ready for the meeting with his Lord at any moment . . . This teaching – a marriage between mysticism and law – has made Ghazālī the most influential theologian of medieval Islam' *(Historical Outlines of Classical Sufism,* Chapel Hill, p.95).

Where lies the truth? And, in that context, what has this book to contribute? This is not the place to examine the whole issue in detail, but it can be said without much hesitation, without implying that all of al-Ghazālī's teachings are in the same vein, that what is presented here indeed invites us to live a life in accordance with the Sharī'ah, with heart fully alive and present, so that it remains whole and healthy, pure and free from evil, worthy of going to its Lord, without any shame or disgrace upon it. It helps us interiorise the externals. More specifically, it enables us to breathe life into the dry bones of rites and rituals which have lost much of their meaning and purpose as they are performed by hearts which have hardened due to the passage of time. (al-Ḥadīd, 57: 16) However, to look briefly at some aspects of the much larger issues at the heart of the controversy may be worthwhile.

That our personality and life have many dimensions can hardly be disputed. We have an external dimension; and an inner one, too. The crux of the issue is what they are, where they should be placed, how they should be related to each other. Must they stand apart, or in conflict? Must there always be a split, leading to friction and antagonism or seclusiveness, between the inner and the outer, the body and spirit, the surface and depth, the form and meaning, the law and love, the Sharī'ah and the *Ṭarīqah?* Are they totally unrelated? Or, are they not two sides of the same coin, two strands of the same existence, the warp and the weft of the fabric of life? Do they not overlap or interact mutually? Can they not reinforce each other? Should the internal not necessarily manifest as the external, and the exterior not become interiorised? These are crucial questions.

Unless these questions are answered properly and right answers found in the light of the Quran and the *Sunnah,* the dangers are real: error may set in and the real objectives of Islam may be in jeopardy. One may eclipse, displace, begin denigrating the other. It is only when one becomes solely concerned with either aspect or extolls one at the cost of the other that extremist reaction takes place.

On the one hand, there have been people whose exclusive concern with the outward details of the law, their love of things worldly, their relations with the corrupt wielders of power, their total identification with the established structures, their fossilisation of the Divine guidance under the crust of legal formalism, their waywardness and decadence drove many to split the inward and outward and stress the inner dimension to the point of decrying the outward forms laid down by the Shari'ah. It is such people about whom al-Ghazālī says: 'those who are so learned about rare forms of divorce can tell you nothing about the simpler things about the spiritual life, such as the meaning of sincerity towards God or trust in Him' (Watt: *Muslim Intellectuals,* p.113). But there have not been many like them, especially in the era in which the issue is regarded to have been most acute. Mālik, Abū Ḥanīfa, Shāfi'ī, Aḥmad, Ja'far Ṣādiq – the jurists *par excellence* – find pride of place in Farīduddīn 'Attār's classical *Tadkhirah al-Awliyā'.* And there is no limit to such names.

On the other hand, there have been some tendencies, gleefully picked up and blown out of all proportion by some Western observers, to belittle or discard the outward forms – the creed, the rites, the code; but they also have been few and exceptional. Those who claimed 'spiritual sovereignty over the logical and ritual forms of religion' (Cragg: *The Mind of the Qur'ān,* p. 180), or who could 'repudiate pilgrimage as an unnecessary rite, when he was to himself a better *Ka'bah.* Or . . . could readily identify the meticulous worshipper in his *Salāt* as no better than an idolator clinging to the invisible and imprisoned in the tangible' (Cragg, p. 168), were never part of the mainstream. They and those who, like Abu Sa'īd ibn Abī al-Khayr, could say:

'Not until every mosque beneath the sun
Lies ruined, will our holy work be done;
And never will true Musalmān appear
Till faith and infidelity are one.'

(R. A. Nicholson, *The Mystics of Islam,* p.90.)

did not echo the voice of an overwhelming majority of Sufis. Indeed almost all the leading Sufis – like 'Abdul Qādir Jīlānī, Shahābuddin Suhrawardī, Abū Ahmad Chishtī, Ahmad Sirhindī – emphatically stressed the absolute need of observing the 'outward': without obedience one cannot get near to Allah.

Just as *fuqahā,* were Sufis, the leading Sufis were pillars of *fiqh.* To mention a few names: Hasan Baṣrī, Sufyān Thūrī, Da'ūd Ṭā'ī, 'Abdullāh ibn Mubārak.

'"The Law without the Truth", says Hujwīrī, 'is ostentation and the Truth without the Law is hypocrisy. Their mutual relation may be compared to that of body and spirit: when the spirit departs from the body, the living body becomes a corpse, and the spirit vanishes like wind. The Moslem profession of faith includes both: the words, 'there is no god but Allah' are the Truth, and the words, 'Mohammed is the apostle of Allah', are the Law; anyone who denies the truth is an infidel, and anyone who rejects the law is a heretic'". (Nicolson, pp. 92-3). No other words can so succinctly sum up the mutual relation of the 'inward' and 'outward'. Ibn Taimīya, whose image is that of a great anti-Sufi, wrote in the same vein.

That 'It is the life of the heart that matters' is true; but only partly. Firstly, as al-Hujwīrī so beautifully explains, the heart without life is as good as dead, but life cannot exist unless it has a heart and the heart needs a body. So they are interdependent; one cannot be affirmed and asserted to the negation of the other. Secondly, they interact. The 'outer' always has a deep impact on the 'inner' and penetrates into the inward depths. One can always see how certain words and deeds cause inner anguish or happiness. Similarly, the 'inner' must pour out through the 'outer'.

Jalāluddīn Rūmī, the famous Sufi poet, in his *Mathnawī* brings his peculiar wisdom to illuminate these very aspects.

Let us remain aware that Rūmī's thought shows varying, even contradictory, strands of thought. (Are we not all at some time or other, totally engrossed in one aspect or the other or in a part-truth? But we, perhaps, take enough care not to show our contradictions, whereas a poet, like Rūmī, gives vent to all his emotions and thoughts, whatever they may be.) Dwelling upon the relationship between the acts and words and the inner states of heart and soul, he says:

> 'Act and word are witnesses to the hidden mind; from these twain infer the inward state.
>
> Know that the probity of the witnesses must be established; the means of establishing it is a (great) sincerity; Thou art dependent on that.
>
> In the case of the word-witness, 'tis keeping thy word (that is the test); in the case of the act-witness, 'tis keeping thy covenant (to perform these acts).
>
> The word-witness is rejected if it speaks falsely, and the act-witness is rejected if it does not run straight.
>
> Thou must have words and acts that are not self-contradictory, in order that thou mayest meet with immediate acceptance.'
>
> (*The Mathnawī,* Vol. VI, R. A. Nicholson (tr.), pp.17-18.)

External beauties are of no avail without internal depths:

> 'The body that hath defect in its spirit will never become sweet (even) if you smear it with honey.' (Ibid., p. 38.)

But if there is beauty inside, the 'outer' is sure to reflect it:

> 'If my heart had a modest disposition, my handsome face would produce naught but purity (goodness).' (Ibid., p. 42.)

To traverse the Way, deeds are essential:

> 'Therefore the Prophet said, "For the purpose of (traversing) this Way there is no comrade more faithful than works. If they be good they will be thy friends for

ever, and if they be evil they will be (as) a snake in thy tomb.'" (Ibid., p.65.)

Rūmī does no more than express what the Quran, in many places, has made abundantly clear, that the 'inward' and the 'outward' are essential to each other. Prayer and humbleness go together: 'Successful are the believers who *in* their Prayers are humble.' (al-Mu'minūn, 23:1) One who 'spends his wealth to purify himself – not as payment for favours received, only longing to seek the face of his Lord the Most High' (al-Layl, 92:18-20) will receive the pleasure of his Lord. Fasting has been enjoined 'that you may become God-fearing.' (al-Baqarah, 2:183) Whosoever performs Pilgrimage and 'honours God's sacred symbols, that is of the godliness in his heart.' (al-Ḥajj, 22: 32) Sacrificing animals is an act of worship, but 'the flesh of them shall not reach God, neither their blood, but godliness from you shall reach Him.' (al-Ḥajj, 22:3)

There can be little doubt that the Inheritance of the Garden of Bliss is for those who come with a heart, pure and whole; but equally important is to meticulously follow the footsteps of the Prophet, upon him be peace. Says the Quran: 'If you love God, follow me and God will love you and forgive you your sins.' (Āl 'Imrān, 3:31)

The observance of the *Ḥudūd* is no less important: 'Those [laws of inheritance] are God's bounds. Whoso obeys God, and His Messenger, him will He bring into gardens through which rivers flow, therein to abide forever; that is a triumph supreme. But whoso disobeys God, and His Messenger, and transgresses His bounds [*Ḥudūd*] him He will commit unto fire, therein to abide forever; and for him there awaits a shameful suffering'. (al-Nisā', 4:13-14)

In conclusion, let me say, I find that nothing illuminates this crucial problem – its diverse aspects, the need and importance of giving due care to both the 'inner' and 'outer', the dependence and interaction of each upon the other; how hearts can be moved by words and actions, how words and actions must be transformed as light shines in hearts which have been overtaken by the love of God – than the following verse of the Quran:

'Is he whose breast God had opened wide unto total self-surrender unto Him, so he walks in a light from his Lord (like the hard of heart)?

Woe, then, unto those whose hearts are hardened against the remembrance of God!

They are lost in manifest error!

God has sent down the best teaching as a Book, consistent within itself, repeating in manifold forms – whereat shiver the skins of those who fear their Lord; then their skins and their hearts soften to the remembrance of God. That is God's guidance, whereby He guides whomsoever He will; and whomsoever God leads astray, no guide has he.'(aI-Zumar, 39:22-3)

I hope the above reflections will put these selections from al-Ghazālī's *Iḥyā'* in their proper perspective. So beautifully translated by my brother Muhtar Holland, they will surely help countless young men and women of our times. They are now making afresh their acquaintance with Islam, rapidly growing in their commitment to Allah and His Messenger, striving harder and harder to bring themselves – their hearts, minds and lives, both private and public – under the sovereignty of one God, as well as the human society and man- kind. It will help them perform their worship rites, prescribed by Islam, in a way, and with such inner states of heart, that they will find great enrichment and receive those immense inner resources without which their *Jihād* – both personal and social – can neither find acceptance in the sight of God, nor yield the results in this world. Such books do not require a critical evaluation of the validity and authenticity of each and every statement and anecdote. What is important is the inspiration and guidance that remain with the reader. And to that end, I trust this book will be extremely useful and merit acceptance in the eyes of Allah.

I pray to Allah *subḥānahū wa ta'ālā* to bless our humble efforts with His acceptance and grace and forgive our acts of omission and commission.

The Islamic Foundation, Leicester,
Jumāda al-Ūlā 1403
March 1983

Khurram Murad
Director General

Translator's Foreword

Even in its external forms alone, the Islamic mode of worship has held a profound fascination for outside observers down through the ages. Many an imagination has been captured by the haunting sound of the Call to Prayer: 'Allāhu Akbar! Allāhu Akbar! . .', or by the stunning spectacle of row upon row of worshippers bowing and prostrating themselves in perfect unison during Friday Congregation in the concourse of some splendid yet at the same time starkly simple Mosque. The cafés and restaurants of a great Muslim city, almost completely deserted in the daylight hours of Ramaḍān, make an eerie impression on travellers who arrive in the Month of Fasting. But it is probably the Pilgrimage, with the aura of mystery and even danger surrounding the 'forbidden cities' of Makka and Madina, that has cast the greatest spell on the minds of those who look at Islam from without.

To Muslims, it is essentially unsurprising that outsiders should find the Islamic forms of worship so intriguing. For we believe Islam to be the 'natural religion' of mankind, as old as our first father Adam – peace be upon him – and as young as the latest infant born into this world. In our own day, the secret of this is revealing itself to growing numbers of men and women beyond the confines of what is regarded, historically and politically, as the World of Islam.

The call to worship none but Allah, the One Almighty God, and to follow the guidance of His noble and blessed Messenger, Muhammad, is being sounded unceasingly on many levels, on countless wavelengths. People hear and respond in very different ways. Sometimes there is a sudden flash of inspiration, sometimes a long and gradual maturing of knowledge and understanding, leading one day to certain conviction. An opening of the feelings may precede rational comprehension. Dreams and visions may play their part. These remarks are based on the experience of many close friends and acquaintances who have come to embrace Islam, as well as on my own. In most cases I know of, an attraction to the Islamic forms of worship has been an important element, if not the principal factor, in the crucial decision to make a full commitment to the religion.

A French lady never forgot the sound of the Call to Prayer, which she had heard as a child in North Africa, and the day came when she knew she must answer it. My friend Robert was a medical student when we travelled together in Turkey many years ago; he could not resist joining the Muslim Congregation at Prayer in the Mosques. I know him now as Dr Abdarrahman. I could fill the page with the names of Muslim brothers and sisters who observed the Fast during Ramaḍān even before they embraced Islam, not to mention the many non-Muslim friends who have recently begun to fast (and who like to give Alms at the end of the fasting month). To speak of myself, I knew in my heart at least fifteen years before I embraced Islam that I must one day visit the Ka'ba in Makka as a Pilgrim. Throughout that time I performed the Islamic ablutions every morning and often at other times as well. Like others with whom I joined in exercises of a spiritual nature, 'receiving' from beyond the influence of heart and mind, I would sometimes feel the movements of the Islamic Prayer arising spontaneously in my body. These and a host of other experiences, culminating in a remarkable vision of the Prophet Muhammad, upon him be peace, together with his noble Companions, eventually convinced me that I *was* a Muslim – however imperfect – and that I ought to acknowledge the fact.

Genuine seekers of Truth can never be satisfied with outer forms alone, even if they believe those forms to have been established by Divine decree. In what is probably his most famous saying, the blessed Prophet himself declared: 'Actions are valued according to intentions.' Indeed, the Beautiful Names of Allah include both 'The Outer (*al-Ẓāhir*)' and 'The Inner (*al-Bāṭin*)'. The need for a greater understanding of the inner dimensions of Islamic worship is acutely felt, not only by a host of potential Muslims but also by many who have lived their whole lives as members of the Islamic community. Few

Muslim authors have written so helpfully on this subject – in any age – as Imām al-Ghazālī. The following pages offer no more than selections, in English translation, from his great work *Iḥyā' 'Ulūm al-Dīn* ('Bringing Religious Knowledge to Life.') I can only pray that they will bring benefit to many, by God's leave, and that none will be misled by errors I may have committed.

New York, 1403/1983 **Muhtar Holland**

1
The Prayer

ṢALĀT

In the Name of God, the Merciful, the Mercy-giving.

(Bismi-llāhi-lraḥmāni-lraḥīm.)

All praise belongs to God, Who has lavished His favours on His servants, filling their hearts with the light of religion and its duties, sent down from the Throne of Glory to the heaven of this world by the steps of mercy. One mark of His compassion: in contrast to earthly kings, though majesty and might belong to Him Alone, He urges the people to bring Him their requests and pleas, saying: 'Will anyone call, that I may answer him? Will anyone seek My forgiveness, that I may forgive him?' Unlike the rulers of this world, He keeps an open door and does not screen himself away. He allows His servants to converse with Him intimately in their Prayers, under all circumstances, be they in Congregation or in isolation. Not merely allowing, indeed, He gently urges and invites. How different are those feeble worldly kings, who grant an audience only when they have received a gift or bribe!

Glory be to Him, therefore, so grand in His sublimity, so Strong in His authority, so Perfect in His graciousness, so All-embracing in His goodness. Blessings and salutations to Muhammad, His chosen Prophet and selected friend, and to his family and Companions, those keys of right guidance and lanterns in the dark.

* * *

Prayer is the pillar of religion, the mainstay of conviction, the chief of good works and the best act of obedience . . .

EXCELLENT MERITS OF PRAYER

1 Merit of the Call to Prayer *(Adhān)*

Said the Prophet, on him be peace: 'On the Day of Resurrection, three people will find themselves on a ridge of black musk. They will have no reckoning to fear, nor any cause for alarm while human accounts are being settled. First, a man who recites the Quran to please God, Great and Glorious is He, and who leads the Prayer to people's satisfaction. Second, a man who gives the Call to Prayer in a Mosque, inviting people to God, Great and Glorious is He, for the sake of His good pleasure. Third, a man who has a hard time making a living in this world, yet is not distracted from the work of the Hereafter.'[1]

According to other Traditions, the Prophet, on him be peace, said: 'All that hear the Muezzin's cry, be they jinn, human or whatever, will testify for him on the Day of Resurrection.'[2] And: 'The hand of the All-merciful is on the Muezzin's head until he completes his Call to Prayer.'[3]

Commentators say that God, Great and Glorious is He, was referring to Muezzins when He revealed the Quranic Verse:

> 'Who speaks better than one who calls to God and acts righteously?' [Fuṣṣilat, 41:33]
>
> (Wa-man aḥsanu qawlan mimman da'ā ilā-Ilāhi wa-'amila ṣāliḥā.)

The Prophet, on him be peace, also said: 'When you hear the Call, repeat what the Muezzin says.'[4] This is the recom- mended practice, except that on hearing the two sentences beginning 'ḥayya 'alā . . .' ('Come to . . .'), one says: 'There is neither power nor strength save in God' (lā ḥawla wa-lā quwwata illā bi-llāh). The response to 'qad qāmati-lṣalāh' ('Prayer has begun') is: 'May God establish it and preserve it as long as the heavens and earth endure' (aqāmahā-Ilāhu wa-adāmahā mā dāmati-Isamāwātu wa-l'arḍ). At dawn, the Call includes the sentence: 'Prayer is better than sleep,' to which we respond with: 'You have spoken truly and veraciously and given good advice' (ṣadaqta wa-bararta wa naṣaḥta). When the Call to Prayer is over, one says:

> 'O God, Lord of this perfect invitation and firmly established Prayer, endow Muhammad with favour, merit and exalted rank. Raise him to the glorious position You have promised him. You do not break Your promise.'
>
> (Allāhumma rabba hādhihi-lda'wati-Itāmmati wa-Isalāti-Iqā'imati Muḥammadani-Iwasīlata wa-Ifaḍīlata wa-Idarajata-Irafi'a / wa-b'athhu-Imaqāma-Imaḥmūda-Iladhī wa'adtah/ innaka lā tukhlifu-Imī'ād.)

Sa'īd ibn al-Musayyab said: 'If a person performs Prayer in a wilderness, an angel prays on his right and an angel prays on his left. If he also gives the Call to Prayer and the signal to begin, angels perform Prayer behind him in rows like mountain ranges.'

2 Merit of the Prescribed Prayers at Set Times (*Ṣalāt*)

Allah, Exalted is He, says:

> 'Prayers have been prescribed for the believers at set times.'[al-Nisā', 4:103]
>
> (Inna-Iṣalāta kānat 'alā-Imu'minīna kitāban mawqūtā.)

Said the Prophet, on him be peace: 'There are five Prayers which God has prescribed for His servants. For those who perform them properly, without disrespectful omissions, there is a guarantee that God will admit them to Paradise. To those who do not observe them, however, God offers no such guarantee: He may punish them or He may admit them to Paradise, as He wills.'[5]

Said the Prophet, on him be peace: 'The five set Prayers may be compared to a stream of fresh water, flowing in front of your house, into which you plunge five times each day. Do you think that would leave any dirt on your body?' When they replied:

'None at all!' The Prophet, on him be peace, said: 'Indeed, the five Prayers remove sins, just as water removes dirt.'[6]

Other sayings of the Prophet, on him be peace:

'The five set Prayers are an expiation, for there is something amongst them by which major sins are repelled.'[7]

'What distinguishes us from the Hypocrites is our attendance at late night and early morning Prayers, both of which they miss.'[8]

'If a man meets God when he has been negligent of the Prayer, God will pay no attention to his other virtues.'[9]

'Prayer is the pillar of religion; to neglect it is to prepare the downfall of religion.'[10]

'Prayer at the appointed times.'[11] (In answer to the question: 'Which action is the most meritorious?')

'If a man performs the five Prayers, in a proper state of purity and at the times prescribed, they will be a light and a proof for him on the Day of Resurrection. But he who misses them will be resurrected along with Pharaoh and Hāmān.'[12]

'The key to Paradise is ritual Prayer.'[13]

'After the affirmation of His Unity, no duty God has imposed on His creatures is dearer to Him than ritual Prayer. Had anything been dearer to Him than this, it would have become a form of worship for His angels. As it is [each of them performs part of the Prayer,] some bowing, some prostrating themselves, some standing upright and some sitting on their heels.'[14]

'Anyone who deliberately misses a Prayer has forsaken his faith.[15] That is to say, he has virtually been stripped of faith, since its knot has been untied and its pillar has fallen. The [Arabic verb meaning] 'has forsaken . . .' is used idiomatically, much as one might say that a man 'has arrived' when he is very near his destination.

'If someone deliberately omits a Prayer, he ceases to enjoy the protective custody of Muhammad, on him be peace.'[16]

Abū Hurayra, may God be pleased with him, said: 'If someone makes his ablution and does it well, then sets out with the intention of performing the Prayer, he is already in the state of Prayer while on his way to it. With each two steps he takes, a good deed is added to his record and a bad deed is erased from it. So do not linger when you hear the signal that the Prayer is beginning, for the one who is farthest from home will get the greatest reward.' They asked: 'Why is that, Abū Hurayra?' and he said: 'Because of all the steps he had to take.'

According to Tradition: 'Of all a man's actions, the first to be examined on the Day of Resurrection will be the Prayer. If it is found to be complete, it will be accepted of him along with the rest of his works, but if it is found wanting it will be rejected along with the rest of his deeds. '[17]

The Prophet, on him be peace, said: 'Abū Hurayra, command your family to perform Prayer, for God will provide you with blessings too numerous to reckon.'[18]

A scholar once said: 'One who performs Prayer is like a merchant, who does not start making a profit until he has recovered all his capital. In similar fashion, one who performs Prayer gets no credit for supererogatory devotions until he has discharged his basic obligations.'

Abū Bakr, may God be pleased with him, used to say: 'When it is time for Prayer, get up and extinguish the Hellfire you have kindled for yourselves.'

3 Merit of Correct Performance (*Ta'dīl*)

The Prophet, on him be peace, said: 'The prescribed Prayer is like a pair of scales: whoever gives full measure will also receive in full.'[19]

Yazīd al-Riqāshī said: 'The Prayer of God's Messenger, on him be peace, was as even as if it had been perfectly balanced.'[20]

Traditions of the Prophet, on him be peace:

'Two members of my Community may perform the Prayer in such a way that their bowing and their prostration are as one, yet their Prayers may be as far apart as heaven and earth.'[21] (In respect of their humility, that is.)

'God will have no regard, on the Day of Resurrection, for that servant of His who does not straighten his spine between bowing and making prostration. '[22]

'Is he not afraid – he who turns his face around in the Prayer – that God may turn his face into that of a donkey?'[23]

'If someone performs his Prayer at the proper time, makes his ablution correctly, does the bowing and prostration properly and observes due humility, that Prayer will rise up, all bright and shining, and will say: "May God take care of you as you have taken care of me!" But if someone performs his Prayer at the wrong time, without correct ablution, not bowing and prostrating properly and not observing due humility, his Prayer will rise up all dark and gloomy, saying: "May God neglect you as you have neglected me." Then when it has reached wherever God wishes, it will be folded up like an old rag and he will be slapped with it in the face.'[24]

4 Merit of Congregational Prayer (*Jamā'a*)

The Prophet, on him be peace, said: 'The merit of congregational Prayer surpasses that of individual Prayer by twenty-seven degrees.'[25]

According to Abū Hurayra, the Prophet, on him be peace, once noticed that certain people were missing from the Congregation. He said: 'I considered appointing someone else to lead the Prayer, while I went to show my disapproval of those absentees by burning down their houses.'[26] According to another version, he added: 'Any one of them would have joined the Congregation if he had expected to get a marrowbone or a couple of trotters.'

According to 'Uthmān, may God be pleased with him, the blessed Prophet said: 'To perform the late evening Prayer (*'Ishā'*) in congregation is equivalent to spending half the night in vigil, while to perform the dawn Prayer (*Fajr*) in congregation is like keeping vigil throughout the night.'[27]

The Prophet, on him be peace, also said: 'To perform the Prayer in congregation is to fill one's throat with worship.'[28]

Sa'īd ibn al-Musayyab said: 'In all of twenty years, the Call to Prayer has always found me in the Mosque.'

Muhammad ibn Wāsi' said: 'Only three things do I wish for in this world: a brother to set me straight if I get crooked; a livelihood for which I do not have to beg; and a congregational Prayer in which I am relieved of absent-mindedness and which is recorded in my favour.'

Ḥātim al-Aṣamm said: 'I was once too late for congregational Prayer and Abū Isḥāq al-Bukhārī was the only one to commiserate with me. Had I lost a son, more than ten thousand would have offered me their condolences, for people find religious misfortune easier to bear than worldly calamity.'

Ibn 'Abbās, may God be pleased with him and with his father, said: 'If a man hears the crier (Muezzin) and does not respond, he does not wish for good and no good is to be expected of him.'

Abū Hurayra, may God be pleased with him, said: 'Better for a human being to have his ear filled with molten lead, than to hear the Call and fail to respond.'

It is related that Maymūn ibn Mihrān once came to the Mosque, only to be told that the people had all left. He quoted from the Quran: 'Surely we belong to Allāh, and to Him we are surely returning,' then said: 'Truly, the value of this Prayer is dearer to me than the governorship of 'Irāq.'

Said the Prophet, on him be peace: 'If a man performs his Prayers in congregation for forty days, never arriving after the "Allāhu Akbar!" of consecration, God will grant him two absolutions: absolution from hypocrisy and absolution from Hellfire.'[29]

It is said that on the Day of Resurrection a group of people will be assembled, their faces like shining stars. The angels will ask them: 'How did you conduct yourselves in life?' To this they will reply: 'On hearing the Call to Prayer, we used to set about our ablutions, letting nothing else distract us.' Another group will then be assembled, their faces like radiant moons. In answer to the same question, they will say: 'We used to make our ablutions ahead of time.' The next group to be assembled will have faces like the sun. They will say: 'We used to hear the Call to Prayer inside the Mosque.'

It is related that early believers used to commiserate with themselves for three days if they missed the first 'Allāhu Akbar!' and for a whole week if they missed the congregational Prayer altogether.

5 Merit of Prostration (*Sujūd*)

God's Messenger, on him be peace, said: 'The servant has no better means of approaching God than prostration in private.'[30] Also: 'Whenever a Muslim performs a prostration for God's sake, God raises him one degree and absolves him of one offence.'[31]

It is related that a man once said to God's Messenger, on him be peace: 'Pray to God that He may include me among those who enjoy your intercession, and that He may grant me your companionship in Paradise.' The Prophet, on him be peace, replied: 'Help me by making frequent prostration.'[32]

According to another Tradition: 'The servant is never closer to God, Exalted is He, than when he is prostrating himself in worship.'[33] This is the meaning of the words of God, Great and Glorious is He, 'Prostrate yourself and draw near.' [Iqra', 96:19] (Wa-sjud wa-qtarib.) God, Great and Glorious is He, also says: 'Their foreheads show the mark left by prostration.' [al-Fatḥ, 48:29] (Sīmāhum fī wujūhihim min athari-lsujūd.) Some say this refers to the dust that sticks to the brow during the act of prostration, while others say it is the light of humility, shining forth from within. The latter view is more correct. According to yet others, it is the radiance that will shine on their faces on the Day of Resurrection, as a result of their ablution.

The Prophet, on him be peace, said: 'If a human being prostrates himself at an appropriate point in his recitation of the Quran, the devil withdraws, weeping as he says: "Alas! This man was bidden to prostrate himself and he has obeyed, so Paradise is his. I was also commanded to make prostration, but I disobeyed and so Hell is my lot."'[34]

It is told of 'Alī ibn 'Abdullāh ibn 'Abbās that he used to make a thousand prostrations every day. They used to call him the Great Prostrator (al-sajjād).

It is related that 'Umar ibn 'Abd al-'Azīz, may God be pleased with him, never prostrated himself on anything but the bare earth.

Yūsuf ibn Asbāṭ used to say: 'Young men, take advantage of your good health, before you become infirm, for I no longer envy anybody except a man who completes his bowing and prostration in Prayer, now that my own time is too short for that.'

Sa'īd ibn Jubayr said: 'I look to nothing in this world for consolation except to prostration in Prayer.'

'Uqba ibn Muslim said: 'No quality in a man is dearer to God, Great and Glorious is He, than the longing to meet Him. At no moment is a man closer to God, Great and Glorious is He, than when he sinks down in prostration.'

Abū Hurayra, may God be pleased with him, said: 'The servant is nearest to God, Great and Glorious is He, when he prostrates himself in Prayer, so that is the time to make many supplications.'

6 Merit of Humble Adoration (*Khushū'*)

God, Exalted is He, said:

> 'And perform the Prayer in remembrance of Me.' [Ṭā Hā, 20:14]
>
> (Wa-aqimi-Iṣalāta li-dhikrī.)

The Exalted One also said:

> 'Do not be one of those who are neglectful.' [al-A'rāf, 7:205]
>
> (Wa-lā takun mina-Ighāfilīn.)

God, Great and Glorious is He, also said:

> 'Do not approach the Prayer when you are intoxicated, until you know what you are saying.' [al-Nisā', 4:43]
>
> (Wa-lā taqrabū-Iṣalāta wa-antum sukārā ḥattā ta'lamū mā taqūlūn.)

Some say that 'intoxicated' means inebriated by many anxieties, while others say it means drunk on the love of this world. According to Wahb, the meaning is obviously a caution against worldly attachment, since the words 'until you know what you are saying' explain the underlying reason. Many are those who pray without having drunk wine, yet do not know what they are saying in their Prayers!

Said the Prophet, on him be peace: 'If a man performs two cycles of Prayer without the distraction of any worldly thought, all his previous sins will be forgiven.'[35]

The Prophet, on him be peace, also said: 'Prayer is nothing but submissiveness, humility, supplication, sighing and remorse, holding out your hands and saying: "O God! O God!" Otherwise it is abortive.'[36]

In the earlier scriptures, we find these words attributed to God, Glorified is He: 'I do not accept the Prayers of everyone who prays. I accept the Prayers of none but those who are humble before My Majesty, who are not arrogant towards My servants, and who feed the poor and hungry for My sake.'

The Prophet, on him be peace, said: 'Ritual Prayer was made obligatory, Pilgrimage and circumambulation were ordained, and the rites of sacrifice were instituted, all for the purpose of ensuring remembrance of God, Exalted is He. If your heart is devoid of awe and reverence for the One Remembered, who is the *aim* and the *goal,* what is your remembrance worth?'[37]

This advice was given to someone by the Prophet, on him be peace: 'When you pray, pray like a person who is saying farewell,'[38] i.e. saying farewell to himself, to his passions and to his life, before setting off on the journey to his Lord. As God, Exalted is He, says:

> 'O Man, you labour towards your Lord laboriously, and you shall meet Him.' [al-Inshiqāq, 84:6]
>
> (Yā ayyuhā-l'insānu innaka kādiḥun ilā rabbika kadḥan fa-mulāqīh.)

The Exalted One also says: 'Be aware of God, for it is God who teaches you.' [al-Baqarah, 2:282] (Wa-ttaqū-Ilāha wa-yu'allimukumu-llāh.)

God, Exalted is He, says also: 'Be aware of God, and know that you are going to meet Him.' [al-Baqarah, 2:223] (Wa-ttaqū-Ilāha wa'lamū annakum mulāqūh.)

Said the Prophet, on him be peace: 'If a man's Prayer does not deter him from indecency and mischief, he gains nothing from God but remoteness.'[39]

Since Prayer is intimate communion, how can it go with heedlessness? Bakr ibn 'Abdullāh said: 'Human being, if you wish to enter the presence of your Lord without permission, and to speak with Him without an interpreter, you have only to enter!' When someone asked him how this could be he said: 'You do your ablution correctly and enter your prayer-niche . . . There you are! You have entered your Lord's presence without permission and may now speak to Him without an interpreter.'

Said 'Ā'isha, may God be pleased with her: 'God's Messenger, on him be peace, would talk to us and we to him, but when it was time for Prayer it seemed as though he did not know us, nor we him. '[40] This was because they were completely in awe of God, Great and Glorious is He.

The Prophet, on him be peace, said: 'God has no regard for a Prayer in which a man's heart is not present as well as his body.'[41]

When Abraham, God's special friend, got up to pray, the throbbing of his heart could be heard two miles away.

When Sa'īd al-Tanūkhī was praying, tears used to flow incessantly down his cheeks and onto his beard.

God's Messenger, on him be peace, once saw a man playing with his beard during the Prayer, so he said: 'If this fellow's heart was submissive, his organs would also act with humility.[42] It is related that al-Ḥasan noticed a man playing with pebbles as he prayed: 'O God, marry me to the maidens of Paradise!' 'A poor suitor you are,' said al-Ḥasan. 'You propose to the maidens of Paradise while playing with pebbles!'

Someone asked Khalaf ibn Ayyūb: 'Don't the flies bother you so much during your Prayer that you have to chase them away?' But he replied: I do not make a habit of anything that would spoil my Prayer.' When asked how he had acquired such patience, he said: I have heard that culprits patiently endure the Sultan's whip, because this gives them a reputation for being "able to take it." They boast of their patient endurance. Here am I, standing before my Lord in Prayer. Am I going to budge for a fly?'

It is related of Muslim ibn Yasār that, when he wanted to pray, he would say to his family: 'You may talk, for I shall not hear you'. It is said that he was praying one day in the Great

Mosque of Baṣra, when a corner of the building collapsed. This attracted a crowd, but he was quite unaware of what had happened until he had finished his Prayer.

Whenever the time of Prayer approached, 'Alī ibn Abī Ṭālib, may God be pleased with him and ennoble his countenance, used to quake and change colour. They asked him: 'What is the matter with you, Commander of the Believers?' To this he would reply: 'The time has come for a trust which God offered to the heavens and the earth and the mountains, but they refused to carry it; they were wary of it, but I have taken it on.'

It is said of 'Alī ibn al-Ḥusayn that he used to turn pale when he made his ablution. When his family asked him what came over him during his ablution, he would say: 'Do you realise before Whom I wish to stand in Prayer?'

According to Ibn 'Abbās, may God be pleased with him and his father, the Prophet David, God bless him and give him peace, used to say in his intimate Prayers: 'My God, who inhabits Your House? And from whom do you accept the Prayer?' Then God told him by inspiration: 'David, he who inhabits My House, and he whose Prayer I accept, is none but he who is humble before My Majesty, spends his days in remembrance of Me and keeps his passions in check for My sake, giving food to the hungry and shelter to the stranger and treating the afflicted with compassion. His light shines in the sky like the sun. If he invokes Me, I am at his service. If he asks of Me, I grant his request. In the midst of ignorance, I give him discernment; in heedlessness, remembrance, in darkness, light. He stands out among ordinary people as Paradise towers over earthly gardens, its rivers inexhaustible and its fruits not subject to decay.'

It is related of Ḥātim al-Aṣamm, may God be pleased with him, that he said, in answer to a question about Prayer: 'When the time for Prayer is at hand, I make a proper ablution, go to the spot where I intend to pray and sit there till all my limbs and organs are in a collected state. Then I stand up to perform my Prayer, placing the Ka'ba between my brows, the Bridge-over-Hell beneath my feet, Paradise to my right and Hell to my left, and the Angel of Death behind me, thinking all the while that this is my final Prayer. Then I stand between hope and fear. I carefully pronounce "Allāhu Akbar!" Then I recite the Quran harmoniously, bow in humility and prostrate myself submissively. I then sit back on my left haunch, spreading out the top of my left foot and raising my right foot on the toes. I follow this with sincerity. Then I wonder whether or not my Prayer has been accepted.'

Ibn 'Abbās, may God be pleased with him and with his father, once said: 'Two moderate cycles of Prayer, performed in full awareness, are better than a whole night's vigil when the heart is inattentive.'

7 Excellence of the Mosque and Place of Prayer (*Masjid*)

God, Great and Glorious is He, said:

> 'The only ones to frequent God's Mosques shall be those who believe in God and the Last Day . . .' [al-Tawbah, 9:18]
>
> (Innamā ya'muru masājida-Ilāhi man āmana bi-Ilāhi wa-lyawmi-l'ākhir.)

The Prophet, upon him be peace, said: 'If a man builds a Mosque for God's sake, be it no bigger than the hollow where a sand grouse lays her eggs, God will build him a palace in Paradise.'[43]

Other Traditions of the Prophet, on him be peace:

'If a man is fond of the Mosque, God will be fond of him.'[44]

'When one of you enters the Mosque, let him perform two cycles of Prayer before sitting down.'[45]

'He who lives next to the Mosque may not pray outside of the Mosque.'[46]

'The angels bless you as long as you remain sitting in the place where you do your Prayers, saying: "O God, bless him. O God, have mercy on him. O God, forgive him." They keep this up until you need an ablution or leave the place of Prayer.'[47]

'In the latter days, there will be members of my Community who come to the Mosques and sit there in circles. Their talk will be of this world and their love of it. Do not sit in their company, for God has no need of them.'[48]

'God, Great and Glorious is He, has said in one of His Books: "The Mosques are My houses on My earth. My visitors are those who frequent them, so blessed is he who purifies himself in his own house, then visits Me in Mine. For the host has a duty to entertain his guest." '[49]

'If you see a man frequenting the Mosque, you may testify to his faith.'[50]

Sa'īd ibn al-Musayyab said: 'Anyone who sits in the Mosque is actually sitting in the company of his Lord, so he has no right to say anything that is not good.'

It was probably one of the Companions who said: 'Gossip in the Mosque consumes good deeds as animals eat up grass.'

Al-Nakha'ī said: 'They used to maintain that walking to the Mosque on a dark night gave a guarantee of Paradise.' Anas ibn Mālik said: 'If someone installs a lantern in a Mosque, the angels and the bearers of the Heavenly Throne do not cease to beg forgiveness for his sins as long as that lamp continues to illuminate that Mosque.'

'Alī, may God ennoble his countenance, said: 'When a man dies, he is mourned by his place of Prayer on earth and by the place in heaven to which his good deeds have ascended.' Then he recited the verse [referring to Pharaoh and his unbelieving followers]:

> 'Neither heaven nor earth shed a tear over them; nor were they reprieved.' [al-Dukhān, 44:29]
>
> (Fa-mā bakat 'alayhimu-Isamā'u wa-l'arḍu wa-mā kānū munẓarīn.)

Ibn 'Abbās said: 'The earth laments him for forty mornings.' 'Aṭā' al-Khurāsānī said: 'Any spot on earth where a man has made a prostration to God will testify on his behalf on the Day of Resurrection, and will weep for him on the day he dies.' Anas ibn Mālik said: 'If a man remembers God, Exalted is He, on any plot of ground, be it by way of Prayer or other form of remembrance, that plot will boast about it to all the surrounding plots. It will rejoice in the remembrance of God, Great and Glorious is He, to the utmost extent of seven lands.

No man gets up to pray without the earth being embellished for him.' It is also said that any place where people stop for the night will either bless them or curse them in the morning.

INTERNAL PREREQUISITES OF PRAYER: ACTIONS OF THE HEART

The Need for Humility and Conscious Awareness

Many Quranic Verses and Traditions could be cited in evidence of this, including the words of God, Exalted is He:

> 'And perform the Prayer to remember Me.' [Ṭā Hā, 20:14]
>
> (Wa-aqimi-Iṣalāta li-dhikrī.)

The obvious force of the imperative is to make something obligatory.

Since heedlessness is the opposite of remembrance, how can someone who is heedless throughout his Prayer be performing it in remembrance of God? The Exalted One said:

> 'Do not be one of those who are neglectful.' [al-A'rāf, 7:205]
>
> (Wa-lā takun mina-Ighāfilīn.)

Here we have a negative imperative, with the obvious force of a prohibition.

God, Great and Glorious is He, also says:

> '. . . until you know what you are saying.' [al-Nisā',4:43]
>
> (ḥattā ta'lamū mā taqūlūn.)

This explains the reason for debarring those who are intoxicated [from the Mosque], but the term 'intoxicated' applies by extension to those who are wholly preoccupied with temptations and worldly thoughts.

When the Prophet, on him be peace, said: 'The Prayer is nothing but submissiveness and humility . . .' he used a particularly definite and emphatic construction in Arabic.[51]

The Prophet, on him be peace, said: 'If a man's Prayer does not deter him from indecency and mischief, he gains nothing from God but remoteness.' Heedless Prayer does nothing to deter a man from these vices.

The heedless are alluded to in the Tradition: 'Many of those who pray derive nothing from their Prayers except weariness and strain.'[52]

The Prophet, on him be peace, said: 'A man gets credit only for that part of his Prayer of which he is conscious.'[53] This is confirmed by the Tradition: 'When performing the Prayer, one is conversing intimately with one's Lord.'[54] Speaking in a state of heedlessness is certainly not what is meant by intimate conversation with the Lord.

To clarify matters further, let us consider the contrast between ritual Prayer, on the one hand, and *Zakāt*,[55] Fasting and Pilgrimage on the other. A man may pay his Alms without being consciously attentive, yet the very act of parting with money runs counter to greed and is hard on the lower self. The case of Fasting is similar: since it subdues the natural forces and breaks the hold of the passions, which are the tools of God's enemy, Satan, its purpose may well be achieved in spite of heedlessness. As for Pilgrimage, it presents physical hardship and difficulty and involves painful struggle, whether or not its actions are performed in full awareness.

In contrast to these other religious duties, ritual Prayer consists only in remembrance, recitation, bowing, prostration, standing erect and sitting down. As for remembrance, it is proximity to God, Great and Glorious is He, and communion with Him. If its purpose is not conversation and dialogue, it must be a verbal and vocal exercise, set to test the tongue in the same way as the belly and the genitals are tested by abstinence during the Fast, as the body is tested by the ordeals of Pilgrimage, or as one is tested by having to part with beloved money on paying the Alms. Without a doubt, this latter supposition must be wrong, for nothing comes more easily to the heedless than idle tongue-wagging. It cannot, therefore, be a simple physical exercise. The sounds produced are significant only when they form articulate speech. Articulate speech must be expressive of what is in the heart and mind, and this is not possible without conscious awareness.

What is the point of praying: 'Show us the Straight Path,' if one is in a state of absent-mindedness? If it is not intended as a humble entreaty and supplication, why bother with the idle mouthing of the words, especially if it has become a habit?

The purpose of Quranic recitation and expressions of remembrance (at various stages in the ritual Prayer) is undoubtedly praise and glorification, supplication and entreaty, addressed to God, Great and Glorious is He. But the veil of heedlessness screens the heart from Him. Far from seeing or witnessing Him, the heedless worshipper is not even aware of Whom he is addressing, as his tongue moves purely from force of habit. How remote this is from the purpose of ritual Prayer, which was prescribed for the refinement of the heart, the renewal of Divine remembrance, and to secure the knot of faith!

We have been discussing the case of recitation and remembrance, but our strictures in this matter are by no means relevant only to the spoken elements in ritual Prayer, as distinct from the physical postures. As for bowing and prostration, their purpose is definitely veneration. While one could be venerating God, Great and Glorious is He, through one's action, although unaware of Him, one might just as well be unconsciously venerating an idol set before one, or even the wall in front. It then ceases to be an act of veneration and is reduced to mere movement of the back and head, devoid of any hardship that might make it a real test.

Ritual Prayer has been made the chief pillar of religion, the criterion for distinguishing between unbelief and Islam. It takes precedence over the Pilgrimage and other forms of worship. It is unique in having capital punishment as the penalty for its abandonment. I do not believe that ritual Prayer enjoys all this special dignity by virtue of its external motions, unless these are linked to the purpose of intimate communion with God. That is what has priority over Fasting, Zakat, Pilgrimage and so on; indeed, over sacrifices and offerings which entail self-denial through financial outlay. As God, Exalted is He, says:

> 'It is not their flesh nor their blood that reaches God: it is your devotion that reaches Him.' [al-Ḥajj, 22:37]
>
> (Lan yanāla-Ilāha luḥūmuhā wa-lā dimā'uhā wa-lākin yanāluhu-Itaqwā minkum.)

What is meant here by 'devotion' (*taqwā*), is a quality that gains control over the heart, disposing it to comply with the commands it is required to obey.

What, then, of the ritual Prayer, if its actions are without purpose?

* * *

You may say that I am going against the consensus of the jurists, if I make the validity of Prayer dependent on conscious awareness, since they stipulate such attention only at the initial 'Allāhu Akbar!' But the jurists do not concern themselves with the inner life or the way of the Hereafter. Their job is to formulate the outer rules of religion, with reference to external physical behaviour. . . As for what is beneficial to the afterlife, this is beyond the scope of jurisprudence, since no consensus can be claimed.

Sufyān al-Thawrī, an early legal scholar, is reported as saying: 'Without humility and awareness, one's Prayer is invalid.' It is related that al-Ḥasan said: 'Any Prayer performed without conscious awareness is a short cut to punishment.' According to Mu'ādh ibn Jabal: 'A man gets no credit for a Prayer in which he deliberately notices those on his right and left.'

According to an authenticated Tradition, God's Messenger, upon him be peace, said: 'Though he performs the whole Prayer, a man may be credited with no more than one sixth or one tenth of it. A man gets credit only for that part of his Prayer of which he is conscious.'[56] If this had been transmitted on lesser authority, it would surely have become a dogma, so why should it not be taken seriously?

'Abd al-Wāḥid ibn Zayd said: 'The scholars are unanimously agreed that a man gets credit only for that part of his Prayers of which he is conscious.' According to him, there is actually a consensus to this effect.

* * *

In short, conscious awareness is the very spirit of ritual Prayer. Attentiveness to the initial 'Allāhu Akbar!' represents the bare minimum required to keep the spark of this spirit alive. . . Of God we beg His gracious support!

INTERNAL STATES CONDUCIVE TO PERFECTING THE LIFE IN PRAYER

These qualities can be expressed in many ways, but they are well summed up in six words, namely: awareness; understanding; reverence; awe; hope; shame.

AWARENESS

By conscious awareness we mean that state in which one's mind and feelings are in no way distracted from what one is doing and saying. Perception is united with action and speech. Thoughts do not wander. When the mind remains attentive to what one is doing, when one is whole-heartedly involved, and when nothing makes one heedless, that is when one has achieved conscious awareness.

UNDERSTANDING

Understanding the meaning of one's words is something that goes beyond awareness, for one may be conscious of making an utterance, yet not be aware of the meaning of that utterance. What we mean by understanding, therefore, is an awareness that also includes comprehension of the meaning of one's utterance. People differ in this respect, not sharing a common understanding of the Quran and the glorifications.

How many subtleties of meaning we come to understand in the course of ritual Prayer! Things that had never occurred to us before. . .

It is in this context that prayer becomes a deterrent to indecency and mischief, for the understanding it brings is a positive obstacle to vice.

REVERENCE

As for reverence, this is something beyond both awareness and understanding. A man may address his servant in full awareness of his speech, and understanding the meaning of his words, yet without reverence, for reverence is an additional element.

AWE

As for awe, it is over and above reverence. In fact, it represents a kind of fear that grows out of the latter. Without experiencing fear, one will not stand in awe. There is an ordinary fear of things we find repugnant, like scorpions or bad temper, but this is not called awe. What we call awe is the kind of fear we have of a mighty king. Awe is the kind of fear induced by a sense of majesty.

HOPE

As for hope, this is unquestionably something else again. There are many who revere some king or other, and who are in awe of him or afraid of his power, yet do not hope to be rewarded by him. In our Prayers, however, we must hope for the reward of God, Great and Glorious is He, just as we fear His punishment for our faults.

SHAME

As for shame, it is something additional to all the rest, for it is based on the realisation of one's deficiencies and the apprehension of sin. It is quite possible to conceive of reverence, fear and hope, without this element of shame.

MEDICATION CONDUCIVE TO INNER SERENITY

As a believer, one must magnify God, Great and Glorious is He, in fear and in hope and in humble awareness of one's shortcomings. There can be no relaxation in any of this once faith has been achieved, although one's intensity will depend on the strength of one's conviction. Any slackness in prayer is surely caused by mental distraction, divided attention, failure to be whole-hearted in communion and a heedless attitude to worship. Random mental activity is the thing that distracts us from prayer; it must therefore be dispelled so that a feeling of serenity can be acquired. To remove the symptom we must treat the cause, so let us find out where it lies. Stray thoughts may be prompted by something external, or they may arise from within.

As for external causes, our attention is caught by anything that happens to engage our eyes or ears. We begin to take an interest in it. Then one thought leads to another and the process goes on and on. Seeing gives rise to thinking, then one thought becomes the cause of another. Sensory impressions do not divert those whose intention is strong and whose aspiration is lofty, but they inevitably distract the weak. The remedy lies in cutting off these causes by lowering the eyes, praying in a dark room, leaving no distracting objects in front of one, or reducing one's range of vision by praying close up to a wall. One should avoid performing the Prayer on the street, in places where there is artificial decoration and on coloured carpets.

That is why very devout people used to worship in a small, dark cell, where there was just enough room for prostration, for it is easier to concentrate in such conditions. Those who were strong would attend the Mosques, keeping their eyes downcast and confining their gaze to the place of prostration. They considered their Prayers to be perfect when they were unaware of the people to their right and left. Ibn 'Umar, may God be pleased with him and with his father, would allow no object to remain in the place of Prayer, not even a copy of the Quran. He would remove any sword he found there and erase any writing.

Internal causes pose a more serious problem. One's worldly concerns may be many and varied, so that the mind does not dwell on a single subject but keeps flying from one direction to another. To lower the eyes is then of no avail, for plenty of distractions have already got inside. The way to deal with this is to make a deliberate effort to comprehend the meaning of the words one is reciting in the Prayer, concentrating on this to the exclusion of everything else. It is helpful to prepare for this before the initial consecration, by reminding oneself of the Hereafter and that one is standing in communion in the awesome presence of God, Glorified is He, and under His scrutiny. Before consecration for Prayer, one should empty the heart of all its cares, leaving oneself free of potential distractions.

God's Messenger, on him be peace, once said to 'Uthmān ibn Abī Shayba: 'I forgot to tell you to cover up the cooking pots that are in the house, for there should be nothing in the house to distract people from their Prayers.'[57] This is a technique for quietening the mind. If mental agitation is not stilled by this tranquilliser, the only recourse is a purgative that will strike at the deep roots of the malady. That is to say, one must examine the distractions that prevent the attainment of inner serenity. These will undoubtedly be traced to one's pressing concerns, which have become so important simply because of one's base desires. One must therefore discipline the lower self by abstaining from those desires and by severing those ties. Anything that distracts us from Prayer is the adversary of our religion; the army of Satan is the foe. To hold it in check is more troublesome than driving it out, so let us drive it out and be rid of it.

The Prophet, upon him be peace, once prayed while wearing a cloak with an ornamented border, a gift from Abū Jahm. He removed it when he had finished his Prayers, saying: 'Take it back to Abū Jahm, for it distracted me from my Prayer. Bring me Abū Jahm's cloak of coarse wool.'[58] God's Messenger, on him be peace, once had new laces put in his sandals. When their newness attracted his attention during his Prayer, he had them removed and the worn laces put back.[59] According to another Tradition, the blessed Prophet once found himself admiring the beauty of a pair of sandals he was wearing, so he made a prostration and said: 'I have humbled myself before my Lord, Great and Glorious is He, so that He will not be displeased with me.' Then he went out and gave the sandals to the first beggar he met. He then told 'Alī, may God be pleased with him, to buy him a worn pair of tanned leather sandals, which he put on his feet.[60]

Before it was declared unlawful for men to wear gold, the Prophet, upon him be peace, used to wear a gold ring on his finger. As he stood in the pulpit one day, he threw this ring away, saying: 'It distracted me: a glance towards it and a glance towards you.'[61]

It is related that Abū Ṭalḥa once prayed in his garden where there were trees. He was attracted by the sight of a honey bird and he spent so long following the movement of the bird, as it flew about seeking an opening in the foliage, that he forgot how many cycles of Prayer he had completed. He told God's Messenger, on him be peace, about the temptation to which he had succumbed, then said: 'Messenger of God, I offer my garden as a charity. Dispose of it as you wish.'[62] According to a different source, he was distracted by the pleasant sight of the bees, buzzing around the fruit as he prayed in his garden. He mentioned this to 'Uthmān, may God be pleased with him, saying 'I offer it as a charity. Use it for the sake of God, Great and Glorious is He.' 'Uthmān then sold the garden for fifty thousand.

Such conduct was intended to eradicate causes of mental distraction and to atone for deficiencies in Prayer. This medicine tackles the root of the disease; it is the only effective remedy. As for the gentler measures we proposed, such as calming oneself and concentrating on understanding the words used in Prayer, they may be useful when passions are feeble and cares are only marginally distracting. But it is useless to try and calm oneself when the pressure of desire is strong, for it will attract you and you will attract it until it gets the better of you. You will be caught up in this process throughout your Prayer.

Consider this analogy: There was a man beneath a tree. He wished to collect his thoughts, but the sparrows disturbed him with their chirping. He would chase them with a stick and then resume his train of thought, but the sparrows would come back and he would have to scare them away with the stick once again. Eventually someone told him: 'This is like being a slave at the wheel, going round and round forever. If you want to escape the vicious circle, you should fell the tree.' So it is with the tree of base desires. Thoughts are attracted to its ramifying twigs and branches, just like sparrows to real trees. Flies are attracted by filth and chasing them becomes a full-time occupation, for they just keep coming back. Random thoughts are like flies.

Our base desires are numerous and human beings are seldom free of them. They all share a common root, namely love of this world. That is the origin of every fault, the basis of every shortcoming, the source of all corruption. Filled with the love of this world, a person becomes so attached to it that he fails to make provision for the Hereafter. He then has no hope of experiencing the pure bliss of communion in Prayer. Those who delight in this world can take no delight in God, Glorified is He, nor in communion with Him. A man aspires to that which gives him joy, so if his pleasure lies in this world he will surely seek it there. Nevertheless, one must continue to strive, turning the heart back towards prayer and reducing the causes of distraction.

This is bitter medicine, so bitter that we instinctively recoil from taking it. The sickness remains chronic and the disease becomes incurable. Great men have endeavoured to perform two cycles of Prayer without having any internal conversation about worldly matters, only to find themselves unequal to the task. No hope, then, for the likes of us! If only we may be safe from temptation during half of the Prayer, or one third, so that our deeds are at least a mixture of good and bad!

In short, the worldly and spiritual aspirations in the human heart are like water poured into a cup full of vinegar; as water goes in, an equal volume of vinegar inevitably goes out and the two can never combine.

INNER STATES AT EACH STAGE OF THE RITUAL PRAYER

THE CALL TO PRAYER

When you hear the Call to Prayer given by the Muezzin, let yourself feel the terror of the Summons on Resurrection Day. Prepare yourself inwardly and outwardly to respond, and to do so promptly. Those who are quick to answer this call are the ones who will be summoned gently on the Day of the Great Review. So review your heart now: if you find it full of joy and happiness, eager to respond with alacrity, you can expect the Summons to bring you good news and salvation on the Day of Judgment. That is why the Prophet, on him be peace, used to say: 'Comfort us, Bilāl!' For Bilāl was the Muezzin and Prayer was the joy and comfort of the Messenger, on him be peace.

RITUAL PURITY

When attending to ritual purity in the things that envelop you in progressively closer layers – your room, then your clothes, then your skin, – do not neglect your inner being, which lies at the heart of all these. Endeavour to purify it with repentance and remorse for your excesses, and a determined resolution not to commit them in future. Cleanse your inner being in this way, for that is the place to be examined by the One you worship.

COVERING PRIVATE PARTS

You cover the private parts, i.e. prevent certain areas of the body from being exposed to human view. But what about the shameful areas of your inner being, those unworthy secrets of your soul, that are scrutinised only by your Lord, Great and Glorious is He? Be conscious of these faults. Be discreet about them, but realise that nothing can be hidden from the sight of God, Glorified is He. Only through repentance, shame and fear, will they be forgiven . . .

FACING THE QIBLA

As for facing the Qibla, in doing so, you turn your external face away from all other directions and toward the House of God,

Exalted is He.* Do you then suppose you are not also required to turn your heart away from everything else, directing it towards God, Great and Glorious is He? What an absurd notion, since this is the whole object of the exercise! The Prophet, on him be peace, said: 'When a man stands up to pray, directing his desire, his face and his heart towards God, Great and Glorious is He, he will come out of that Prayer as on the day his mother gave him birth.'[63]

STANDING UPRIGHT

As for standing upright, it means holding oneself erect – in body and spirit – in the presence of God, Great and Glorious is He. Your head, which is the highest member of your body, ought to be bowed down as a reminder of the need to keep the heart meek and humble, free of haughtiness and pride . . .

INTENTION

When forming the intention, resolve to be responsive to God, Great and Glorious is He, by performing the Prayer in obedience to His command, by doing it properly, by avoiding things that invalidate or mar it, and by doing all this sincerely for the sake of God, Great and Glorious is He, in hope of His reward and in fear of His punishment, seeking His grace and favour by His leave. . .

TAKBĪR

As for the takbīr,† your heart must not gainsay the words on your tongue. If you feel in your heart that there is something greater than God, Glorified is He, though your words are true, God will attest that you are a liar . . .

OPENING INVOCATIONS

When making the opening invocation,‡ be very wary of disguised polytheism in yourself. It was concerning those who

---

* i.e. towards the Ka'ba.

† Affirmation of God's Supreme Greatness, in the words: ' Allahu Akbar!'

‡ The author refers to the invocation that includes the words: 'I am no polytheist.' His caution is equally appropriate, however, if one recites the invocation ending: 'There is no god but You.'

worship for the sake of human as well as Divine approval that God, Exalted is He, revealed the Verse:

> 'Whoever hopes to meet his Lord, let him do righteous work and let no one share in the worship due to his Lord.' [al-Kahf, 18:110]
>
> (Fa-man kāna yarjū liqā'a rabbihī fa-lya'mal 'amalan ṣāliḥan wa-lā yushrik bi-'ibādati rabbihī aḥadā.)

When you say: 'I take refuge with God from accursed Satan', you should be aware that the devil is your enemy and that he is waiting for an opportunity to alienate you from God, Great and Glorious is He. Satan is envious of your ability to commune with God, and to prostrate yourself before Him...

RECITING THE QURAN

Where recitation of the Quran is concerned, we can distinguish three types of people: (a) those who move their tongues unconsciously; (b) those who pay conscious attention to the movement of the tongue, understanding the meaning while listening as if to a person outside themselves; this is the degree of 'those on the right'; (c) those who start from awareness of the meaning, then use the tongue to give expression to this inner consciousness. The tongue may act as interpreter for the inner feeling, or as its teacher. In the case of those nearest to God, the tongue is an interpreter. . .

BOWING DOWN

According to 'Ikrima, God, Great and Glorious is He, is referring to the postures of standing, bowing, prostration and sitting, when He says:

> '. . . Who sees you when you stand up [to pray] and your movements among those who prostrate themselves.' [al-Shu'arā', 26:218-219]
>
> (Alladhī yarāka ḥīna taqūmu wa-taqallubaka fī-lsājidīn.)

Bowing (*rukū'*) and prostration (*sujūd*) are accompanied by a renewed affirmation of the supreme greatness of God, Glorified is He. . .

In bowing, you renew your submissiveness and humility, striving to refine your inner feeling through a fresh awareness of your own impotence and insignificance before the might and grandeur of your Lord. To confirm this, you seek the aid of your tongue, glorifying your Lord and testifying repeatedly to His supreme majesty, both outwardly and inwardly.

Then you rise from bowing, hopeful that He will be merciful towards you. To emphasise this hope within you, you say: 'sami'a-llāhu liman ḥamidah,' meaning: 'God hears those who give thanks to Him.' Acknowledging the need to express gratitude, you immediately add: 'Rabbanā laka-lḥamd' – 'Grateful praise to You, our Lord!' To show the abundance of this gratitude, you may also say: 'mil'u-lsamāwāti wa-mil'u-l'arḍ' – 'as much as the heavens and earth contain.'

PROSTRATION

Then you go down in prostration. This is the highest level of submission, for you are bringing the most precious part of your body, namely your face, down to meet the most lowly of all things: the dust of the earth. If possible, you should make your prostration directly on the bare ground, this being more conducive to humility and a surer sign of self-abasement. When you place yourself in this position of lowliness, you should be aware that you belong there. You are restoring the branch to its root, for of dust you were created and to dust you shall return. At the same time you should renew your inner awareness of God's majesty, saying: 'Glory to my Lord Most High!' (Subḥāna rabbiya-l'a'lā.) Repeat this to add confirmation, for saying it only once is not sufficiently emphatic.

When your inner feeling has clearly been refined, be confident in hoping for God's mercy. For His mercy quickly flows towards weakness and lowliness, not towards arrogance and vanity.

As you raise your head, say 'Allāhu Akbar!' and ask for what you need, making the supplication of your choice, e.g. 'My Lord, forgive and have mercy! Overlook my faults, of which You are well aware!' (Rabbi-ghfir wa-rḥam wa-tajāwaz 'ammā ta'lam.)

You then make a second prostration, reinforcing your submissiveness.

SITTING AND TESTIFYING

When you sit up to make the testimony (*tashahhud*), sit decorously. Declare that all the prayers and good works you perform are for the sake of God, and that everything belongs to Him. Such is the meaning of *al-taḥīyyāt*. . . . Be inwardly aware of the Prophet, on him be peace, and of his noble person, as you say: 'Peace be upon you, O Prophet, as well as God's mercy and blessings.' (Salāmun 'alayka ayyuhā-lnabīyu wa-raḥmatu-llāhi wa-barakātuh.) Be sure that your salutation will reach him, and that he will return an even more perfect greeting to you. Then salute yourself and all God's righteous servants. Then testify to the Unity of God, Exalted is He, and to the Mission of Muhammad, His Prophet, on him be peace. By repeating this two-fold testimony, you reaffirm the covenant of God, Glorified is He, and assure yourself of its protection.

END OF SUPPLICATION

At the end of your ritual Prayer, you should offer a traditional supplication, imploring and entreating with meekness and humility, confidently hoping to be heard. Let your supplication include your parents and the other believers.

SALUTATION

Finally, and with the intention of concluding your Prayer, address your salutation (*salām*) to the angels and to the others present. Feel a sense of gratitude to God, Glorified is He, for having enabled you to complete this act of worship. Imagine that you are saying farewell to this Prayer of yours, and that you may not live to see another like it. . .

STORIES OF THE HUMBLE, MAY GOD BE PLEASED WITH THEM, AND THEIR PRAYERS

It should be known that humility is the product of faith and the result of conviction, brought about by the majestic power of God, Great and Glorious is He. Those blessed with it are humble not only in their Prayers, but at other times also, even when they are on their own or when they need to use the toilet. For humility is caused by the awareness that we are always in the sight of God, by awareness of His majesty and by awareness of our human failings. It is by consciousness of these things that humility is engendered, so it is not confined to ritual Prayers.

There was once a man, we are told, who never held his head up to the sky in all of forty years; so great were his modesty and humility before God, Glorified is He.

Some people assumed that al-Rabī' ibn Khaytham must be blind, because he always lowered his head and kept his eyes half-closed. For twenty years he was a regular visitor to the home of Ibn Mas'ūd. When the latter's maidservant saw him, she would say to her master: 'Your blind friend is here.' Ibn Mas'ūd used to laugh when she said this. Whenever she went to answer the guest's knock at the door, she would see him with his head down and his eyes averted. Ibn Mas'ūd would look at him and say, quoting from the Quran:

> 'And give good tidings to the humble.' [al-Ḥajj, 22:34]
>
> (Wa-bashshiri-lmukhbitīn.)

Then he would add: 'By God, if the Prophet, on him be peace, had seen you, he would have been so pleased with you!' (In one version of this story, the wording is 'he would have loved you,' and in another: 'he would have laughed.') One day, he was walking with Ibn Mas'ūd when they passed the blacksmith's workshop. He fell in a faint at the sight of the bellows and the fire blazing in the furnace. Ibn Mas'ūd sat with him till the time of Prayer, but he did not come round. He then carried him home, where he remained unconscious till twenty-four hours after having fainted, so missing all five Prayers. Ibn Mas'ūd stayed close by him, saying: 'By God, this is real fear!'

Al-Rabī' used to say: 'When engaged in Prayer, I never pay attention to anything, except what I am saying and what is being said to me.'

'Āmir ibn 'Abdullāh was one of those who are humble in their Prayers. He would sometimes pray while his daughter was playing the tambourine and the women of the house were chattering freely, but he was quite insensitive to the noise and did not even hear it. They once asked him: 'Does anything come into your mind during the Prayer?' 'Yes,' said he, 'the thought that I am standing in the presence of God, Great and Glorious is He, and that I am bound for Paradise or for Hell.' He was then asked: 'Do you get any worldly thoughts, as we do?' To this he replied: 'I would rather be made a butt for lances than get that sort of thing in my Prayer.' He was also in the habit of saying: 'Even if the veil was lifted from the unseen, my faith could not be more certain than it is now.'

Another of these characters was Muslim ibn Yasār, the one who did not notice the collapse of a column while he was praying in the Mosque.

One of these men had a gangrenous limb. Amputation was necessary, but it seemed impossible until someone said: 'He won't feel a thing while he is at Prayer.' The operation was, in fact, successfully performed during the Prayer.

Someone said: 'Prayer belongs to the Hereafter; to enter it is to leave this world.' Another was asked if he had any worldly thoughts during his Prayers. 'Neither in my Prayers nor at any other time,' said he. Yet another was asked: 'Do you remember anything during the Prayer?' He replied: 'Is anything dearer to me than the Prayer, that I should recall it while I am praying?'

Abūl Dardā', may God be pleased with him, used to say: 'The sensible thing is to attend to one's needs first, so as to have nothing on one's mind when approaching the Prayer.'

Some of them would keep their Prayers short, fearing the whisperings of the devil. We are told that, on a certain occasion, 'Ammār ibn Yāsir finished his Prayer rather quickly. When someone commented on this, he said: 'Did you see me skip any of the essentials?' The answer was: 'No!' He then explained: 'I was forestalling the distraction of Satan. God's

Messenger, on him be peace, said: "Though a man performs the whole Prayer, he may get no credit for half of it, or a third, a quarter, a fifth, a sixth or a tenth. A man gets credit only for that part of his Prayer of which he is conscious."'[64]

It is said that Ṭalḥa and al-Zubayr were among a group of the Companions, may God be pleased with them, who were particularly noted for keeping their Prayers brief. They explained that they followed this practice in order to forestall the whisperings of Satan.

It is related that 'Umar ibn al-Khaṭṭāb, may God be pleased with him, said from the pulpit: 'A man's whiskers may turn grey in Islam, without his having completed one Prayer for God, Exalted is He.' When the people asked him how this could be, he said: 'Because he never achieves perfect humility, submissiveness and devotion to God, Great and Glorious is He, in any of his Prayers.'

Abūl 'Āliya was once asked about the words of God, Exalted is He:

> 'Those who are heedless of their Prayers.' [al-Mā'ūn, 107:5]
>
> (Alladhīna hum 'an ṣalātihim sāhūn.)

He said: 'This refers to those who are so heedless in their Prayers that they do not know whether they have performed an even number of cycles or an odd one.' According to al-Ḥasan, it refers to those who heedlessly let the time for Prayer slip by. Others say: 'This is directed at those who are neither happy when they pray on time, nor sorry when they are late in praying. They see no virtue in promptness and no sin in delay.'

Said Jesus, on him be peace: 'God, Exalted is He, says: "Through obligatory duties My servant attains salvation. Through supererogatory devotions My servant draws close to Me."'

The Prophet, on him be peace, said: 'God, Exalted is He, says: "My servant does not achieve salvation except by fulfilling the duties I have set him."'[65]

It is related that the Prophet, on him be peace, once omitted a verse from the part of the Quran he recited in the course of a ritual Prayer. As he was turning to leave, he said:

'What did I recite?' Nobody spoke, so he repeated the question to Ubayy ibn Ka'b, may God be pleased with him, who said: 'You recited such-and-such a Sūra, omitting a particular verse. We are wondering whether it has been abrogated or taken out.' The Prophet, on him be peace, said: 'Good for you, Ubayy!' Then he turned to the others and said: 'What are we to make of people who come for their Prayers, line up in their rows behind their Prophet, but do not know what he is reciting to them from the Book of their Lord? That is just how the Children of Israel behaved, so God, Great and Glorious is He, spoke to their Prophet through inspiration, saying: "Tell your people: 'You present your bodies before Me and you offer Me your tongues, but you keep your hearts from Me. What you are doing is futile.'"'[66]

* * *

These stories and Traditions help to prove that the fundamental elements in ritual Prayer are humility and conscious awareness, and that merely going through the motions, in a state of heedlessness, has little value for the life hereafter. God knows best. We pray for His gracious help and guidance.

2

Almsgiving

*ZAKĀT**

God, Exalted is He, has made Zakat, (Almsgiving) one of the pillars of Islam and has usually mentioned it immediately after the Prayer, saying, 'And perform Prayer and give Alms'. The Prophet, upon him be peace, said: 'Islam rests on five things: to witness that there is no god but God and that Muhammad is His servant and Messenger, to perform Prayer, to give Alms . . .'. God, Exalted is He, has warned those who do not give Zakat with dire consequence, for He says: 'Those who amass gold and silver and do not spend them in the way of God – give them the glad tidings of a painful chastisement' [al-Tawbah, 9:34]

Certain inward attitudes and duties are incumbent on those who seek, through payment of their Alms, the way that leads to the Hereafter:

1 Understand the Purpose and Significance

To understand the necessity and significance of paying the Alms, how it represents a test of character, and why it has been made one of the fundamentals of Islam, even though it is a financial transaction and not a physical act of worship.

Three points deserve consideration here:

(a) *TESTING THE DEGREE OF LOVE FOR GOD*

To pronounce the two sentences of the Confession of Faith (*Shahāda*) ('There is no god but God – Muhammad is God's

---

* Zakat (or Zakah) is the amount of Alms which must be paid annually by every Muslim possessing more than a certain amount of wealth. The root meaning of the Arabic term suggests that it is a means of purification and development.

Messenger') is obligatory as affirmation of the Divine Unity and testimony to the singleness of the One to Whom all worship is due. Complete fulfilment of this obligation requires that he who affirms the Divine Unity should direct his love to none but the One, the Unique, for love tolerates no partnership. There is little value in mere verbal affirmation. The degree of love is tested only by separating the lover from other things he loves.

Now, worldly goods are an object of love in everybody's eyes, being the means by which they enjoy the benefits of this world; because of them they become attached to life and shy away from death, even though death leads to meeting the Beloved. The truth of our claim to love God is therefore put to the test, and we are asked to give up the wealth which is the darling apple of our eye.

That is why God, Exalted is He, said:

> 'God has bought from the believers their persons and their goods, Paradise being theirs for the price.' [al-Tawbah, 9:111]
>
> (Inna-llaha-shtarā mina-lmu'minīna anfusahum wa-amwālahum bi-anna lahumu-ljanna.)

This concerns Jihād, the struggle in the way of God, which entails a readiness to sacrifice even life itself in longing to meet God, Great and Glorious is He. The renunciation of wealth is trivial by comparison.

Once this concept of testing the degree of love is understood to underlie the spending of wealth and material sacrifice, people fall into three groups in this respect:

Firstly, those who affirm the Divine Unity, fulfil their covenant and renounce all their worldly goods, setting aside neither pounds nor pence. They are unwilling to incur the liability to pay the Alms; so much so that when one of them was asked the amount due on two hundred dirhams, he replied: 'For ordinary people the legal requirement is five dirhams, but we must give up everything.'

Thus Abū Bakr, may God be pleased with him, donated all his wealth, while 'Umar, may God be pleased with him, gave half of his. When the Prophet, upon him be peace, said to the latter: 'What have you kept for your family?' he replied: 'An equal amount.' And when he asked the same question of Abū Bakr, may God be pleased with him, he said: 'God and His Messenger.' The Prophet, upon him be peace, then said: 'The difference between you is the difference between your two answers.'[1] For Abū Bakr, the veracious, had borne himself out completely, keeping nothing back for himself but the Beloved, i.e. God and His Messenger.

Secondly, at a lower level are those who hold on to their goods, waiting for occasions of need and seasons of charity. Their object in saving up is to supply their own needs, without extravagance, and to devote what is left over to charitable purposes as the occasion may arise. Such people do not confine their giving to the prescribed amount of the Alms. One group of the Successors[2] (the generation following the Companions, may God be pleased with them) maintained the view that wealth is subject to other dues apart from the Zakat. When al-Sha'bī was asked if this was the case, he replied: 'Yes, have you not heard the words of God, Great and Glorious is He:

> "[True piety means . . .] and giving away one's wealth, much as one loves it, to close relatives, orphans, the wayfarer and beggars, and for the emancipation of slaves . . ." [al-Baqarah, 2:177]?'
>
> (Wa-ātā-lmāla 'alā ḥubbihī dhawī-lqurbā wa-lyatāmā wa-lmasākīna wa-bna-lsabīli wa-lsā'ilīna wa-fī-lriqāb.)

They cited the words of God, Great and Glorious is He:

> 'And spend from what We have provided them with.' [al-Baqarah, 2:3]
>
> (Wa-mimmā razaqnāhum yunfiqūn.)

as well as His words, Exalted is He:

> 'And spend from that which We have provided you.' [al-Munāfiqūn, 63:10]
>
> (Wa-anfiqū mimmā razaqnākum.)

They maintained that these duties, far from being abrogated by the 'Verse *of zakāt'** form part of the mutual obligations of all Muslims. In other words, whenever a well-to-do Muslim encounters one who is in need, it is incumbent upon him to relieve that need, over and above his payment of the Alms.

The correct legal opinion in this matter is that the relief of pressing need is a collective duty, resting on the Community as a whole, since a Muslim cannot be allowed to perish.

It may be argued that a well-to-do person is not obliged to pay for the relief of want except by way of a loan, and that no donation can be required of him once he has discharged his due by giving his Alms. It could also be argued that he is never- theless required to make a donation and that lending is impermissible, i.e. it is not permissible to burden the poor with the acceptance of a loan. There is no unanimity on this question.

Thirdly, to resort to lending is to descend to the final level of ordinary people. Those who belong to this third group confine themselves to the bare fulfilment of duty, neither more nor less. This is the lowest degree, the limit to which all ordinary people confine themselves because of their miserliness, their attachment to money and the feebleness of their love of the Hereafter, As God, Exalted is He, said:

> 'If He were to ask your possessions of you, and press you to give most of them, you would be miserly.' [Muḥammad, 47:37]
>
> (In yas'alkumūhā fa-yuḥfikum tabkhalū.)

What a difference between a servant whose property and person God has bought, with Paradise as the price, and one He does not even ask to give all of it because he is so miserly!

(b) *ELIMINATION OF MISERLINESS*

The Divine decree by which God, Glorified is He, bids His servants to expend their wealth, is also significant in respect of

* Quran (al-Tawbah, 9:60), in which specific recipients of the Zakat are mentioned.

purging the habit of miserliness, which is one of the deadly sins. As the Prophet, on him be peace, said: 'Three are deadly: avarice indulged, passion pursued and self-conceit.'[3] And in the words of God, Exalted is He:

> 'Those who are shielded from their own greed, they are the ones who will prosper.' [al-Ḥashr, 59:9]
>
> (Wa-man yūqa shuḥḥa nafsihī fa-ulā'ika humu-lmufliḥūn.)

The habit of miserliness is only eliminated by making oneself accustomed to spending money, for to break an attachment one must force oneself away till a new habit is formed.

From this point of view, therefore, Zakat signifies purgation, in that he who pays the Alms is purged of the deadly evil of miserliness. The purity he acquires is in proportion to his outlay, to his delight in giving away and to his joy in spending for the sake of God, Exalted is He.

(c) *EXPRESSION OF GRATITUDE*

The third factor is gratitude for benefits received, for the servant is indebted to God, Great and Glorious is He, for bounties both personal and material. Bodily acts of worship are an expression of gratitude for bodily blessings, while financial acts of worship express gratitude for material bounty. How mean one must be to see a poor man in needy straits, and yet be unwilling to give up two-and-a-half or ten per cent of one's wealth in token of one's gratitude to God, Exalted is He, for sparing one the need to beg as others must.

2 Payment at Proper Time

The second duty concerns the time of payment. One of the good practices of religious people is to anticipate the moment when payment falls due, demonstrating their willingness to comply by bringing joy to the hearts of the poor, forestalling the obstacles time might place in the way of charitable action, aware that there are dangers in delay as the servant runs the risk of disobedience should he postpone beyond the appointed moment. Whenever the impulse to good arises from within, the opportunity must be grasped at once as heaven-sent. 'The believer's heart lies between two fingers of the All-merciful.' Yet how fickle is the heart! The Devil threatens poverty and bids us to commit atrocious and abominable deeds. Demonic suggestion follows hard on the heels of angelic inspiration. One should therefore seize the opportunity and fix a definite month for giving the Alms (if one is used to paying it all at once.) One should endeavour to choose one of the most propitious times, resulting in extra closeness to God and compounding the value of the Zakat.

Such a favourable time would be the month of Muḥarram, since it is the first in the year and one of the Sacred Months; or Ramaḍān, for the Prophet, on him be peace, was the best of all creatures, and during Ramaḍān he was as unstinting as the breeze that blows.[4] Ramaḍān also enjoys the special virtue of the Night of Destiny, as well as being the month in which the Quran was sent down. Mujāhid used to say: 'Do not say "Ramaḍān," for Ramaḍān is one of the Names of God, Exalted is He. Rather say: "the month of Ramaḍān."' Dhūl Ḥijja is also one of the months of great merit; as well as being a Sacred Month, it is distinguished by the major Pilgrimage, the *Ḥajj,* and the Well-known Days (the first ten of the month) and the Numbered Days, which are the days of *tashrīq.**

3 Give in Secret

The third duty is secrecy, for this is farthest removed from hypocritical display and reputation-seeking. Said the Prophet, on him be peace: 'The most meritorious form of Almsgiving is the effort to help a poor man, made in secret, by one who is himself of little means.'[5] According to one of the scholars: 'Three things are accounted among the treasures of righteousness, one of them being to give Alms in secret.' This saying has also been attributed to the Prophet, on him be peace.[6] The Prophet, on him be peace, also said: 'Let the servant do a

---

* The three days following the day of sacrifice on the tenth. Tashrīq, 'turning to the East,' is usually understood as referring to the sun-drying of the sacrificial flesh.

good deed in secret and God will surely record it to his credit as a secret; if he reveals it, it will be transferred from the secret list and recorded among good works done openly; if he talks about it, it will be taken off both lists and recorded as hypocrisy.'[7] According to the well-attested Tradition: 'Seven will God shade on the day when there will be no shade but the shade of His Throne: one of them is a man who offers Alms without his left hand knowing what his right hand has given.'[8] In another Tradition: 'Secret Alms extinguish the anger of the Lord.'[9] God, Exalted is He, said:

> 'But if you hide it and give it to the poor, it is better for you.' [al-Baqarah, 2:271]
>
> (Wa-in tukhfūhā wa-tu'tūhā-lfuqarā'a fa-huwa khayrun lakum.)

The advantage of secrecy is that it confers deliverance from the perils of hypocritical ostentation and reputation-seeking. As the Prophet, on him be peace, said: 'God does not accept from a braggart, a hypocrite or one who always looks for gratitude.'[10] He who talks about Almsgiving is seeking prestige, while he who gives for all the world to see is after public recognition; these pitfalls are avoided by secrecy and silence. Some have taken such an extreme view of the merit of secrecy as to maintain that the recipient should not know the identity of the giver. Some used to slip their Alms into the hand of a blind man, while others would drop them in a poor man's path or in the place where he sat, so that he could see the gift without seeing the giver. Some would tuck their Alms in the poor man's clothes while he was sleeping; still others would convey them by way of a third party so as to hide the donor's identity, the intermediary being asked to keep the secret and charged not to disclose it.

Such measures were designed to extinguish the anger of the Lord, Glorified is He, and as a precaution against hypocrisy and reputation-seeking. Whenever it is inevitable that at least one person should be in the know, it is preferable to entrust the Alms to an agent for delivery to the needy beneficiary, who should not be known to his benefactor; for knowing the beneficiary carries the double danger of ostentation and expectation of gratitude, whereas knowing the intermediary carries the former alone.

Whenever fame is the donor's objective, his work will be in vain, since the purpose of Almsgiving is to eliminate miserliness and to weaken the love of wealth. But the love of status has a stronger hold over the soul than the love of wealth, and both of them have deadly consequences in the Hereafter. In the tomb, while the attribute of miserliness will assume, as it were, the form of a stinging scorpion, the attribute of ostentatiousness will turn into a viper. We are bidden to render them both weak or to kill them, so as to ward off their mischief or at least reduce it. But whenever we seek recognition and renown it is just like reinforcing the viper at the scorpion's expense: as the scorpion gets weaker so does the snake get stronger. Things would have been better left as they were. The way to reinforce those attributes is to act in accordance with their demands, while the way to reduce their power is to combat and oppose them and to act counter to their demands. So what is the use of going against miserly impulses only to yield to hypocritical motives, weakening the lesser only to reinforce the more powerful?

4 Give Openly

The fourth duty, when one knows that such conduct will tend to encourage others to follow suit, is to let one's giving be seen. In doing so, however, one must be inwardly on guard against hypocritical motives.* God, Great and Glorious is He, has said:

> 'If you make your Almsgiving public, it is well . . .' [al-Baqarah, 2:271]
>
> (In tubdū-lṣadaqāti fa-ni'immā-hī.)

That is, in cases where display is called for, either to set a good example or because a beggar has made his request in public. In the latter instance it is not proper to withhold Alms

* The author mentions that the remedy for hypocrisy is discussed elsewhere in his work, *Iḥyā*, viz. in *Kitāb al-Riyā'*.

for fear of publicity; rather should one give while making every effort to be inwardly on guard against hypocrisy. This is because, apart from the expectation of gratitude and the risk of hypocrisy, there is a third danger in visible Almsgiving, namely that of offending a poor man's dignity. It may be hurtful to him to be seen to be needy. But someone who begs in public is bringing the disgrace upon himself; there is therefore no sense in being wary.

Consider similar cases: It is forbidden to expose a person's vice so long as he keeps it private, and it is equally prohibited to spy on him and gossip about it. A flagrant offender, on the other hand, has only himself to blame when he suffers the penalty of public disgrace. Of like import are the words of the Prophet, on him be peace: 'He who casts off the garment of shame has no cause to complain of slander.'[11]

God, Exalted is He, said:

> 'And spend of that which We provide for them, in secret and in public' [al-Ra'd, 13:22]
>
> (Wa-anfaqū mimmā razaqnāhum sirran wa-'alāniya.)

He commends giving in public also, because this has the advantage of encouraging others. His servant should therefore take careful stock, weighing this benefit against the risks involved, for the situation varies from case to case and from one individual to another. For certain people under certain conditions open giving is preferable. To one who is aware of the pros and cons, and whose vision is unclouded by desire, what is right and proper in any given case will be readily apparent.

5 Avoid Taunting and Hurting

The fifth duty is not to invalidate one's Alms through taunting and hurting. As God, Exalted is He, said:

> 'Do not make your Almsgiving void by taunting and hurting.' [al-Baqarah, 2:264]
>
> (La tubṭilū ṣadaqātikum bi-lmanni wa-l'adhā.)

There is some disagreement as to the true meaning of taunting and hurting. According to some, taunting is reminding a person of a favour, while hurt lies in making it commonly known. Said Sufyān: 'Anyone who taunts invalidates his Alms.' When they asked him the nature of taunting, he replied: 'Reminding him of the favour and talking about it.' According to others taunting is to exploit a person in return for a gift, while hurt lies in making him feel ashamed of his poverty. Still others say that taunting means making one's gift an excuse for arrogant behaviour, while hurt is caused by scolding and rebuking a man for begging.

The Prophet, on him be peace, said: 'God does not accept the Alms of a taunter.'[12]

My personal opinion is that taunting has its root and origin in the conditions and qualities of the heart, from which it then ramifies into external manifestations on the tongue and other organs. It stems from seeing oneself as the bountiful benefactor, whereas one ought really to look upon the poor person as one's own benefactor, by virtue of the fact that he accepts what one owes to God, Great and Glorious is He, and allows one to attain purity and salvation from the Fire. Had he not accepted, one would have remained under obligation. One is therefore indebted to the poor person inasmuch as he makes the palm of his hand a surrogate for God, Great and Glorious is He, to collect what is due to Him. God's Messenger, on him be peace, said: 'Alms fall into the hand of God, Great and Glorious is He, before they reach the hand of the beggar.'[13]

One should therefore realise that giving Alms is actually paying God, Great and Glorious is He, what is due, while the poor man is actually receiving his sustenance from God, Exalted is He, to whom it has first passed. Suppose a man owed someone a debt, and that he transferred it to a servant totally dependent on him for his livelihood; that servant would be a silly fool to believe that the creditor was obliged to him for making the repayment. The true benefactor would be the man responsible for his livelihood. As for him, he is merely discharging a liability incurred in getting what he wanted; since he is pursuing his own interests, why should he think he is doing someone else a favour?

Anyone who grasps the significance of the three points we mentioned earlier, while discussing the purpose and importance of the Zakat – or even one of them – must realise that he is a benefactor only to himself, through expending his wealth either to demonstrate his love of God, Exalted is He, or to purge himself of the vice of miserliness, or to give thanks for the blessing of wealth in the hope of receiving more.

However that may be, there is no problem between the donor and the poor recipient until the former comes to regard himself as a benefactor. But should he be so foolish as to see himself in this light, he then begins to manifest all the symptoms of taunting we have described; talking about his donation and advertising it, seeking recompense in the form of gratitude, good wishes, service, respect and veneration, attention to his interests, deferential treatment and sub-servience in all matters. All these things are the fruits of taunting, the inner nature of which we spoke about earlier.

As for hurtfulness, its outward manifestations are scolding, derision, coarseness of speech, frowning, humiliation by exposure, and every type of ridicule. Its inner source is twofold: (i) reluctance to part with money and the painfulness of the experience, which inevitably causes bad temper, and (ii) regarding oneself as better than the poor man and considering him inferior by reason of his need. Both attitudes stem from ignorance.

Reluctance to part with money is stupidity, for one must be stupid indeed to resent laying out one coin in exchange for the equivalent of a thousand. The outlay is known to be made in the hope of earning the approval of God, Great and Glorious is He, and reward in the abode of the Hereafter, a nobler aim than to spend or to have spent either to purge oneself of the vice of greed or to give thanks in the hope of receiving more. However one views it, there can be no justification for reluctance.

As for the supercilious attitude, this is also a sign of ignorance. One who recognised the superiority of poverty over wealth, and who was aware of the danger to the rich, would surely not despise the poor; rather would he seek their blessing and wish he were at their level. The righteous among the rich will enter Paradise five hundred years later than the poor. That is why the Prophet, on him be peace, said: 'By Lord of the Ka'ba, they are the greatest losers.' When Abū Dharr asked: 'Who are they?' he replied: 'Those with the most wealth . . .'[14] Besides, how could one despise the poor, when God, Exalted is He, has made them a source of profit? One strives to acquire wealth and increase it, and tries to keep as much of it as one needs. Then one is obliged to hand over to the poor in accordance with their needs, withholding any surplus that would be detrimental. Thus the rich are gainfully employed in providing for the poor, from whom they are distinguished only by having wrongs to settle, problems to cope with and surpluses to take care of until they die, when their enemies will devour what they leave behind.

When reluctance is transformed and gives way to joy and gladness at being helped by God, Exalted is He, to pay one's due and to discharge one's obligation through its acceptance by the poor, there is then no more hurtfulness with its scolding and frowning; instead, there is happiness, appreciation and gratitude.

Although we have explained the source of taunting and hurting, you may well say: 'Seeing oneself in the role of benefactor is somewhat vague. Is there some indicator, some test to apply to the heart in order to make sure one is not regarding oneself as a benefactor?' Yes, there is indeed a precise and unambiguous indicator. Suppose, for instance, that a poor man committed an offence against you, or teamed up with an enemy of yours. Would your disapproval and antipathy be all the greater if you had previously given Alms to the man? If the answer is yes, then your Almsgiving was not untainted by resentment, since it has caused you to expect more of him than you would otherwise have done.

This too may seem vague. You may say: 'Nobody's heart is detached from that sort of thing, so what is the remedy for it?' Well, it does have a remedy, both internally and externally. The internal remedy is to become conscious of the truths we have already mentioned: understanding the necessity of the Almsgiving and coming to see that the beneficiary is the real benefactor, in that by his acceptance he enables us to purge ourselves.

As for the external remedy, this consists of some particular good deeds performed by the one who is prone to taunting, for well-intentioned actions have a good influence on the heart. This is why some people used to place their Alms in front of a poor man and stand before him, begging him to accept them, so that they assumed the role of beggars and felt how they would hate to be rejected. Others used to spread their palms, so that the poor man's hand would be uppermost when he took from them. Whenever 'Ā'isha and Umm Salama, may God be pleased with them, sent a gift to a poor person by messenger, they would tell the messenger to memorise the person's good wishes, then they would wish him the same, saying: 'This in return for that, so that our Almsgiving may be pure.' Such people did not look for good wishes, for these represent a kind of compensation, and so they matched each wish with its equal. 'Umar ibn al-Khaṭṭāb followed the same practice, as did his son 'Abdullāh, may God be pleased with them both. Spiritual specialists in purifying hearts used to treat their hearts this way.

Externally, there is no remedy apart from these good deeds, signifying self-abasement, humility and appreciativeness, while internally the cure lies in the awareness and understanding we have mentioned. It is a matter of action on the one hand, of knowledge on the other. There is no treatment for the heart except the medicine of knowledge and action.

This condition applies to Almsgiving just as humility does to Prayer. The proof is to be found in the words of the Prophet, on him be peace: 'A man profits from his Prayer only to the extent that he does it consciously;'[15] and: 'God does not accept the Alms of a taunter;'[16] as well as in the words of God, Great and Glorious is He: 'Do not make your Almsgiving void by taunting and hurting.' [al-Baqarah, 2:264]*

6 Adopt Humility

The sixth duty is to think little of one's donation, for to regard it highly is to invite that sanctimonious pride which is one of the deadly sins, making good deeds worthless. The Exalted One said:

---

* As for the legalistic ruling, according to which payment of the Zakat is valid and effective even if this condition is not fulfilled, that is another story.

'And on the battle-day of al-Ḥunayn, when you were so proud of your numerical strength, it helped you not at all.' [al-Tawbah, 9:25]

(Wa-yawma ḥunaynin idh a'jabatkum kathratukum fa-lam tughni 'ankum shay'ā.)

It is also said that whenever an act of obedience is belittled, it is magnified in the sight of God, Great and Glorious is He, while a sin considered serious appears small in His eyes. Another saying has it that three things are necessary to make a kindness complete: thinking little of it, doing it promptly, and keeping it out of sight.

To make much of a gift is not the same as taunting and hurting, however. A man who spent his money on the construction of a Mosque or hospice might well think it something to boast of, but taunting and hurting would be out of the question. Sanctimonious pride and self-importance do tend to infect all acts of worship, and their antidote is knowledge and action.

As for knowledge, it must be recognised that ten or two-and-a-half per cent* is a tiny fraction, and that to pay only this is to content oneself with the least generous level of expense, as we have explained above. This is something to be ashamed of rather than to boast about. Even if one rose to the highest level, disbursing all or most of one's wealth, one should still reflect on where it came from in the first place, and for what purpose it is being spent. For all wealth belongs to God, Great and Glorious is He. It is to Him one should be grateful for being given it and being enabled to spend it, so why pride oneself on spending for the sake of God, Exalted and Glorified is He, what is actually His property all along? And, if one's situation is such that one must look to the Hereafter, spending for the sake of spiritual reward, why boast of giving what one expects to receive many times over?

As for action, one's giving should be done with a sense of shame at one's meanness in holding back the rest of one's wealth from God, Great and Glorious is He. One's demeanour should be humble and abashed, like that of someone who is

* The standard rates of Zakat on wealth and produce respectively.

asked to hand back a deposit but returns only part of it and holds on to the rest. For all wealth belongs to God, Great and Glorious is He, and He would prefer to see us give all we possess. If He has not commanded His servants to do so, it is only because that would be too hard on them by reason of their greed. As God, Great and Glorious is He, has said: 'Were He to press you to give all of it, you would be miserly.' [Muḥammad, 47:37]

7 Give the Best and the Dearest

The seventh duty is to select from one's wealth what is best and dearest to one – the finest and most excellent part – for God, Exalted is He, is Good and accepts only what is good. If the offering has been acquired by dubious means, it may not strictly belong to the donor and will then be disqualified. According to the Tradition reported by Abān on the authority of Anas ibn Mālik: 'Blessed is the servant who spends out of wealth he has earned without sin.'[17] Not to make the offering from the best one has is to be guilty of bad manners, since it means that one is keeping the best for oneself, for one's servant or for one's family, and so preferring others over God, Great and Glorious is He. To treat a guest in this fashion, offering him the worst food in the house, would be sure to annoy him.

That is to look at it from the standpoint of God, Great and Glorious is He. If we look to ourselves and to reward in the Hereafter, no sane person is going to put others before himself. Whatever we possess, we may either give it in Alms and so make it truly ours to keep, or consume it for some immediate purpose and say goodbye to it forever. But it is unreasonable to concentrate solely on the present, neglecting to lay by for the future. God, Exalted is He, said:

> 'You who believe, spend from the good things you have earned, and of what we have produced for you from the earth, and do not choose the bad part to donate when you would not take it yourselves without turning your noses up at it.' [al-Baqarah, 2:267]

(Yā ayyuhā-lladhīna āmanū anfiqū min ṭayyibāti mā kasabtum wa-mimmā akhrajnā lakum mina-l'arḍi wa-lā tayammamū-lkhabītha minhu tunfiqūna wa-lastum bi-ākhidhīhi illā an tughmiḍū fīh.)

That is to say, you would accept it only reluctantly and with a feeling of shame, so do not select it for your Lord.

According to the Tradition: 'A single coin may overtake a hundred thousand.'[18] This happens when a person's offering represents the best and finest part of his wealth, and is made in a spirit of pleasure and happiness in giving. Were he to offer a hundred thousand times as much, but out of the part of his fortune he disliked, that would only go to show that he would not offer to God, Great and Glorious is He, anything he was fond of. That is why God, Exalted is He, finds fault with people who set aside for Him what they themselves dislike. He said, Exalted is He:

'They set aside for God what they themselves dislike, and their tongues expound the lie that the better portion will be theirs. No . . .' [al-Naḥl, 16:62]

(Wa-yaj'alūna lillāhi mā yakrahūna wa-taṣifu alsinatuhumu-lkadhiba anna lahumu-lḥusnā lā.)

Some Quran-reciters pause at this negation, stressing the falsehood of what those people say, before continuing with:

'. . . doubt about it: theirs is the Fire.'

(. . . jarama anna lahumu-lnār.)

That is, they have earned the Fire by setting aside for God what they themselves dislike.

8 Seek the Worthy and Deserving

The eighth duty is to seek out a truly worthy recipient for one's offering (*ṣadaqa*), rather than be content with just anybody who happens to fall within the eight categories of legally qualified beneficiaries. For among those generally eligible there are some with special qualities. Attention should be paid to these special qualities, which are six in number:

Firstly, one should seek out those pious people who have renounced the world and devoted themselves exclusively to the business of the Hereafter. The Prophet, on him be peace, said: 'Partake of no food but that of a pious man; and let none but the pious partake of your own.'[19] The reason for this is that your food will support the pious person in his piety; by helping him, you will become a partner in his worship. The Prophet, on him be peace, also said: 'Offer your food to the pious, and favour the believers with your kindness.'[20] Another version has the words: 'Treat to your food those whom you love in God, Exalted is He.'[21]

A certain scholar used to make a point of feeding poor Ṣūfīs to the exclusion of others. When it was put to him that he ought rather to distribute his charity among the poor in general, he replied: 'No, these are people entirely devoted to God, Glorified is He. If smitten with destitution, one of them might be distracted, so to revive one man's devotion to God, Great and Glorious is He, is dearer to me than giving to a thousand of those whose sole concern is this world.' These words were related to al-Junayd, who expressed his approval and said: 'This man is one of the saints of God, Exalted is He.' He then went on to say: 'It is a long time since I heard better words than these.' It was later reported that this man had fallen upon hard times and had decided to close up his shop, so al-Junayd sent him some money and said: 'Take this as your capital and keep your shop open; commerce is surely not harmful to men like you.' This man was a grocer who used to serve the poor without charging them anything.

Secondly, the recipient should be chosen from among the people of learning, to support him in his quest for knowledge. Learning is the noblest form of worship, so long as it is based on right intention. Ibn al-Mubārak used to address his charity exclusively to people of learning. 'I know of no rank, after that of Prophethood, superior in merit to the rank of the learned. If one of them became preoccupied with his needs he would not be free to devote himself to knowledge and concentrate on study. It is therefore better to give them the freedom to pursue learning.'

Thirdly, the recipient should be sincere in his piety and exclusive worship and devotion to God alone. This singleness of worship and devotion (*Tawḥīd*) is apparent when, on accepting a gift, he offers praise and thanks to God, Great and Glorious is He, regarding Him as the source of the blessing rather than any intermediary. Such a man is truly grateful to God, Glorified is He, recognising that all blessings flow from Him. Luqmān said, in his testament to his son: 'Set no-one as benefactor between yourself and God, but count the favours you receive from others as a liability.'

If anyone gives thanks to other than God, Glorified is He, it is as if he does not know the true Benefactor and does not realise that the intermediary is under compulsion, subject to the will of God, Great and Glorious is He, Who has endowed him with motivation and enabled him to act. The intermediary is therefore under compulsion to give; he could not choose to do otherwise after God, Great and Glorious is He, had instilled in his heart that his well-being both spiritual and worldly depended on his acting. When the impulse becomes powerful it demands a resolute response; it becomes irresistible and brooks no hesitation. It is God, Great and Glorious is He, Who creates these impulses and arouses them to action. It is He Who strips them of weakness and vacillation, compelling the faculties to respond to their demands. No-one conscious of this could pay attention except to the Cause of all causes.

Such an awareness is more valuable to the giver than the praise and thanks he might receive from others, for that would be mostly useless lip-service, whereas the help extended to this truly dedicated servant of God will not be wasted. As for those who lavish praise and good wishes in return for a gift, they may find fault when they are not satisfied and utter curses when they are disappointed, though cases vary.

It is related that the Prophet, on him be peace, once sent an offering to a certain man, telling the messenger to remember anything he might say. This is what the man said on receiving the gift: 'The praise belongs to God, Who neither forgets those who remember Him nor neglects those who thank Him.' Then he added: 'O God, You have not forgotten so-and-so (meaning himself), so let him not forget You.' When news of this reached God's Messenger, on him be peace, he said in delight: 'I knew he would say that.'[22] See how this man confined his attention to God alone.

The Prophet, on him be peace, once said to a man: 'Repent!' The man said: 'I repent to God alone; I do not repent to Muhammad.' To this the Prophet, on him be peace, replied: 'The right has been acknowledged where it is due.'[23]

When it was Divinely revealed that 'Ā'isha, may God be pleased with her, was innocent of the slanderous accusations levelled at her in the Episode of the Lie, Abū Bakr, may God be pleased with him, told his daughter: 'Get up and kiss the head of God's Messenger, God bless him and give him peace.' But she said: 'By God, I shall not do so! I shall give thanks to none but God.' The Prophet, on him be peace, said: 'Leave her alone, Abū Bakr.'[24] According to another version: "Ā'isha, may God be pleased with her, said to Abū Bakr, may God be pleased with him: "The praise is God's, not yours nor that of your friend."' God's Messenger, on him be peace, did not object to what she had said, although it was by his tongue that the Divine revelation had reached her.

To see things as emanating from any source but God, Glorified is He, is the mark of the unbelievers. God, Exalted is He, has said:

> 'And when God alone is mentioned, then contract with aversion the hearts of those who do not believe in the Hereafter, but when those apart from Him are mentioned, see how they rejoice.' [al-Zumar, 39:45]
>
> (Wa-idhā dhukira-llāhu waḥdahu-shma'azzat qulūbu-lladhīna lā yu'minūna bi-l'ākhirati wa-idhā dhukira-lladhīna min dūnihi idhāhum yastabshirūn.)

If someone has not inwardly purified himself of seeing the intermediaries except for what they really are, it is as if his secret soul is still attached to a concealed polytheism. He should therefore devote himself to God, Glorified is He, to purify his affirmation of Divine Unity from the taints and stains of associating others with Him.

Fourthly, the recipient should be a person who has remained anonymous and kept his need to himself, not being given to fuss and complaint; or one of those magnanimous people who, though fortune has departed, still remain unaffected and preserve their high standards. As God, Exalted is He, has said:

> 'The ignorant man accounts them rich because of their restraint, but you shall know them by their mark – they do not beg of men importunately.' [al-Baqarah, 2:273]
>
> (Yaḥsabuhumu-ljāhilu aghniyā'a mina-lta'affufi ta'rifu-hum bi-sīmāhum lā yas'alūna-lnāsa ilḥāfā.)

In other words, they do not make a nuisance of themselves by begging, for they are rich in their certainty and proud in their fortitude. Such men should be sought out by thorough investigation of the religious people in each neighbourhood, and by looking deeply into the circumstances of good and decent people, since the reward for addressing charity to them is many times greater than for spending on those who are vociferous in their begging.

Fifthly, the recipient should be someone saddled with a large family, or else disabled by illness or some other cause, so as to come under the import of the words of God, Great and Glorious is He:

> 'For the poor who are restrained in God's cause.' [al-Baqarah, 2:273]
>
> (Lil-fuqarā'i-lladhīna uḥṣirū fī sabīli-llāh.)

In other words, they are held in confinement on the way of the Hereafter by reason of family responsibilities, hardship or psychological problems.* They 'cannot travel about the earth' [2:273] because their wings are clipped and their limbs are tied. This is why 'Umar, may God be pleased with him, used to give the household of the Prophet, on him be peace, a flock of sheep – not fewer than ten – while the Prophet himself, on him be peace, would suit his gift to the size of the family.[25] 'Umar, may God be pleased with him, was once asked about

* This also refers to those who are restrained from earning their livelihood because they are wholly engaged in striving in the way of God, e.g. Jihad and learning.

the toughest trial and his answer was: 'A big family and little money.'

Sixthly, the recipient should be a close relative, whether paternal or maternal. The offering will then serve the additional purpose of strengthening ties of kinship, the reward for which is incalculable. 'Alī, may God be pleased with him, once said: 'To present one of my brothers with a single coin is dearer to me than giving twenty in Alms, while to present him with twenty is dearer to me than giving a hundred in Alms, and to present him with a hundred is dearer to me than emancipating a slave.' Friends and fellows in a good cause should be preferred over mere acquaintances, just as relatives are put before strangers.

Conclusion

Each of these fine points should therefore be taken into consideration, for they represent the desired qualities. Within each quality there are further gradations, so one ought to seek the highest. If anyone can be found in whom all these qualities are combined, that is the greatest treasure and the supreme prize. If one does one's best and succeeds, one gets a double reward, but even if one fails there is still a single reward for the effort.

One of the two rewards is instant purging of oneself from the attribute of greed, as well as the confirmation in one's heart of the love of God, Great and Glorious is He, and the endeavour to obey Him. These are the qualities that grow even stronger in the heart, making it yearn to meet God, Great and Glorious is He.

The second reward is the benefit derived from the prayers and aspirations of the recipient, for the hearts of the righteous are efficacious both immediately and in the long term. If one succeeds, therefore, both rewards accrue, while if one fails the first is achieved but not the second. Here, as in other instances, the reward for successful endeavour is twofold. But God knows best!

3

Fasting

ṢAWM

Three Grades

It should be known that there are three grades of Fasting: ordinary, special and extra-special.

Ordinary Fasting means abstaining from food, drink and sexual satisfaction.

Special Fasting means keeping one's ears, eyes, tongue, hands and feet – and all other organs – free from sin.

Extra-special Fasting means fasting of the heart from unworthy concerns and worldly thoughts, in total disregard of everything but God, Great and Glorious is He. This kind of Fast is broken by thinking of anything other than God, Great and Glorious is He, and the Hereafter; it is broken by thinking of worldly matters, except for those conducive to religious ends, since these constitute provision for the Hereafter and are not of this lower world. Those versed in the spiritual life of the heart have even said that a sin is recorded against one who concerns himself all day with arrangements for breaking his Fast. Such anxiety stems from lack of trust in the bounty of God, Great and Glorious is He, and from lack of certain faith in His promised sustenance.

To this third degree belong the Prophets, the true saints and the intimates of God. It does not lend itself to detailed examination in words, as its true nature is better revealed in action. It consists in utmost dedication to God, Great and Glorious is He, to the neglect of everything other than God, Exalted is He. It is bound up with the significance of His words:

'Say: "Allāh!" then leave them to their idle prattling.' [al-An'ām, 6:91]

(Quli-llāhu thumma dharhum fī khawḍihim yal'abūn.)

Inward Requirements

As for Special Fasting, this is the kind practised by the righteous. It means keeping all one's organs free from sin and six things are required for its accomplishment:

1 *SEE NOT WHAT DISPLEASES GOD*

A chaste regard, restrained from viewing anything that is blameworthy or reprehensible, or that distracts the heart and diverts it from the remembrance of God, Great and Glorious is He. Said the Prophet, on him be peace: 'The furtive glance is one of the poisoned arrows of Satan, on him be God's curse. Whoever forsakes it for fear of God will receive from Him, Great and Glorious is He, a faith the sweetness of which he will find within his heart.'[1]

Jābir relates from Anas that God's Messenger, on him be peace, said: 'Five things break a man's Fast: lying, backbiting, scandalmongering, perjury and a lustful gaze.'[2]

2 *SPEAK NOT . . .*

Guarding one's tongue from twaddle, lying, backbiting, scandalmongering, obscenity, rudeness, wrangling and controversy; making it observe silence and occupying it with remembrance of God, Great and Glorious is He, and with recitation of the Quran. This is the fasting of the tongue. Said Sufyān: 'Backbiting vitiates the Fast.'[3] Layth quotes Mujāhid as saying: 'Two habits vitiate Fasting: backbiting and telling lies.'

The Prophet, on him be peace, said: 'Fasting is a shield; so when one of you is Fasting he should not use foul or foolish talk. If someone attacks him or insults him, let him say: "I am Fasting, I am Fasting!"'[4]

According to Tradition: 'Two women were Fasting during the time of God's Messenger, on him be peace. They were so fatigued towards the end of the day, from hunger and thirst, that they were on the verge of collapsing. They therefore sent a message to God's Messenger, on him be peace, requesting permission to break their Fast. In response, the Prophet, on him be peace, sent them a bowl and said: "Tell them to vomit into it what they have eaten." One of them vomited and half filled the bowl with fresh blood and tender meat, while the other brought up the same so that they filled it between them. The onlookers were astonished. Then the Prophet, on him be peace, said: "These two women have been Fasting from what God made lawful to them, and have broken their Fast on what God, Exalted is He, made unlawful to them. They sat together and indulged in backbiting, and here is the flesh of the people they maligned!"'[5]

3 *HEAR NOT . . .*

Closing one's ears to everything reprehensible; for everything unlawful to utter is likewise unlawful to listen to. That is why God, Great and Glorious is He, equated the eavesdropper with the profiteer, in His words, Exalted is He:

> 'Listeners to falsehood, consumers of illicit gain.' [al-Mā'idah, 5:42]
>
> (Sammā'ūna li-lkadhibi 'akkālūna li-lsuḥt.)

God, Great and Glorious is He, also said:

> 'Why do their rabbis and priests not forbid them to utter sin and consume unlawful profit?' [al-Mā'idah, 5:63]
>
> (Law-lā yanhāhumu-lrabbānīyūna wa-l'aḥbāru 'an qawlihimu-l'ithma wa-'aklihimu-lsuḥt.)

Silence in the face of backbiting is therefore unlawful. God, Exalted is He, said: 'You are then just like them.' [al-Nisā', 4:140] That is why the Prophet, on him be peace, said: 'The backbiter and his listener are copartners in sin.'[6]

4 *DO NOT . . .*

Keeping all other limbs and organs away from sin: the hands and feet from reprehensible deeds, and the stomach from questionable food at the time for breaking Fast. It is meaningless to Fast – to abstain from lawful food – only to break one's Fast on what is unlawful. A man who Fasts like this may be compared to one who builds a castle but demolishes a city. Lawful food is injurious in quantity not in quality, so Fasting is to reduce the former. A person might well give up excessive use of medicine, from fear of ill effects, but he would be a fool to switch to taking poison. The unlawful is a poison deadly to religion, while the lawful is a medicine, beneficial in small doses but harmful in excess. The object of Fasting is to induce moderation. Said the Prophet, on him be peace: 'How many of those who Fast get nothing from it but hunger and thirst!'[7] This has been taken to mean those who break their Fast on unlawful food. Some say it refers to those who abstain from lawful food, but break their Fast on human flesh through backbiting, which is unlawful. Others consider it an allusion to those who do not guard their organs from sin.

5 *AVOID OVEREATING*

Not to over-indulge in lawful food at the time of breaking Fast, to the point of stuffing one's belly. There is no receptacle more odious to God, Great and Glorious is He, than a belly stuffed full with lawful food. Of what use is the Fast as a means of conquering God's enemy and abating appetite, if at the time of breaking it one not only makes up for all one has missed during the daytime, but perhaps also indulges in a variety of extra foods? It has even become the custom to stock up for Ramaḍān with all kinds of foodstuffs, so that more is consumed during that time than in the course of several other months put together. It is well known that the object of Fasting is to experience hunger and to check desire, in order to reinforce the soul in piety. If the stomach is starved from early morning till evening, so that its appetite is aroused and its craving intensified, and it is then offered delicacies and allowed to eat its fill, its taste for pleasure is increased and its force exaggerated; passions are activated which would have lain dormant under normal conditions.

The spirit and secret nature of Fasting is to weaken the forces which are Satan's means of leading us back to evil. It is therefore essential to cut down one's intake to what one would consume on a normal night, when not Fasting. No benefit is derived from the Fast if one consumes as much as one would usually take during the day and night combined. Moreover, one of the proprieties consists in taking little sleep during the daytime, so that one feels the hunger and thirst and becomes conscious of the weakening of one's powers, with the consequent purification of the heart.

One should let a certain degree of weakness carry over into the night, making it easier to perform the night Prayers (*tahajjud*) and to recite the litanies (*awrād*). It may then be that Satan will not hover around one's heart, and that one will behold the Kingdom of Heaven. The Night of Destiny represents the night on which something of this Kingdom is revealed. This is what is meant by the words of God, Exalted is He:

> 'We surely revealed it on the Night of Power.' [al-Qadr, 97:1]
>
> (Innā anzalnāhu fī laylati-lqadr.)

Anyone who puts a bag of food between his heart and his breast becomes blind to this revelation. Nor is keeping the stomach empty sufficient to remove the veil, unless one also empties the mind of everything but God, Great and Glorious is He. That is the entire matter, and the starting point of it all is cutting down on food.

6 *LOOK TO GOD WITH FEAR AND HOPE*

After the Fast has been broken, the heart should swing like a pendulum between fear and hope. For one does not know if one's Fast will be accepted, so that one will find favour with God, or whether it will be rejected, leaving one among those He abhors. This is how one should be at the end of any act of worship one performs.

It is related of al-Ḥasan ibn Abīl Ḥasan al-Baṣrī that he once passed by a group of people who were laughing merrily. He said: 'God, Great and Glorious is He, has made the month of Ramaḍān a racecourse, on which His creatures compete in His worship. Some have come in first and won, while others have lagged behind and lost. It is absolutely amazing to find anybody laughing and playing about on the day when success attends the victors, and failure the wastrels. By God, if the veil were lifted off, the doer of good would surely be preoccupied with his good works and the evildoer with his evil deeds.' In other words, the man whose Fast has been accepted will be too full of joy to indulge in idle sport, while for one who has suffered rejection laughter will be precluded by remorse.

Of al-Aḥnaf ibn Qays it is reported that he was once told: 'You are an aged elder; Fasting would enfeeble you.' But he replied: 'By this I am making ready for a long journey. Obedience to God, Glorified is He, is easier to endure than His punishment.'

Such are the inwardly significant meanings of Fasting.

Importance of Observing Inward Aspects

Now you may say: 'Suppose someone confines himself to curbing his appetite for food and drink and his sexual desire, to the neglect of these inward aspects. According to the experts in jurisprudence his Fast is valid. So what are we to make of this?'

You must realise that those versed in the external requirements of the law base their formal stipulations on evidence less cogent than the proofs we have advanced in support of these internal prerequisites, especially those relating to backbiting and the like. However, scholars of external legality are concerned only with such obligations as fall within the capacity of ordinary heedless people, wholly caught up in the affairs of this world.

As for those learned in knowledge of the Hereafter, the meaning they attach to validity is acceptance, and by acceptance they mean attainment of the goal. According to their understanding, the goal of Fasting is the acquisition of one of the qualities of God, Great and Glorious is He, namely steadfastness (*ṣamadīya*), as well as following the example of the angels by abstaining as far as possible from the desires of the flesh, for they are immune to such passions. The human status is superior to that of the animals, since man is able by the light of reason to tame his lust; yet it is inferior to that of the angels, in that he is subject to carnality and put to the test in combat with its temptations.

Whenever man falls prey to lust, he sinks to the lowest of the low and joins the animal herd. Whenever he curbs his desires, he ascends to the highest of the high and attains the angelic level. The angels are near the presence of God, Great and Glorious is He, so those who follow their example and model themselves on their character will likewise draw near to God, Great and Glorious is He. To resemble one who is near is to be near. This nearness, however, is not spatial but qualitative.

If this is the secret of Fasting among men of profound spiritual understanding, what benefit is to be derived from postponing a meal only to combine two meals after sunset, while indulging in all other passions the whole day long? If there were any good in such conduct, what could the Prophet, on him be peace, have meant by saying: 'How many of those who Fast get nothing from it but hunger and thirst?'

This is why Abūl Dardā' said: 'How fine is the sleep of the wise and their non-Fasting! Don't they just put to shame the Fasting and wakefulness of fools! A mere atom from those possessed of certainty and true piety is better and weightier than seeming mountains of worship by the misguided.' For the same reason one of the scholars said: 'How many who Fast are not keeping Fast, and how many who do not keep Fast are Fasting!'

The Fasting non-Faster is he who keeps his limbs and organs pure of sin while still eating and drinking; the non-Fasting Faster is he who goes hungry and thirsty while giving full licence to his limbs and organs. Those who understand the significance of Fasting and its secret meaning are aware that he who abstains from food, drink and sexual intercourse, while breaking Fast by involving himself in sin, is like one who performs his ablution by wiping part of his body three times (in compliance with the external legal requirement), yet neglects what is really important, namely the actual washing. Because of this stupidity his ritual Prayer is rejected. By contrast, he who does not abstain from eating, yet does Fast in the sense of keeping his organs free from all that is unworthy, is comparable to one who washes the proper parts of his body only once each. God willing, his ritual Prayer is acceptable, since he has paid due attention to the essentials, even if he has omitted the details. But he who combines the two may be compared to one who not only washes each part of the body, but does so three times each, for he attends to essentials and details alike, and this constitutes perfection.

The Prophet, on him be peace, once said: 'The Fast is a trust, so let each of you keep this trust!'[8] And when he recited the words of God, Great and Glorious is He:

> 'Surely God bids you restore trusts to their owners.' [al-Nisā', 4:58]
>
> (Inna-llāha ya'murukum an tu'addū-l'amānāti ilā ahlihā.)

he touched his ears and his eyes, saying: 'Hearing is a trust and sight is a trust.'[9] If speech were not likewise a trust of the Fast, the Prophet, on him be peace, would not have said: 'Say: "I am Fasting!"' In other words: 'My tongue has been entrusted to my care, so how can I release it to answer your insults?'[10]

It therefore becomes apparent that every act of worship has both an outer and an inner aspect, a husk and a kernel.

4
The Pilgrimage

ḤAJJ

In the Name of God, the Merciful, the Mercy-giving

(Bismi-llāhi-Iraḥmāni-Iraḥīm.)

All praise belongs to God, Who made the affirmation of His oneness a refuge and fortress for His servants; Who made the Ancient House (the Ka'ba) a concourse secure for mankind, ennobled it in honour, virtue and grace by attribution to Himself, and made the visitation and circumambulation of it a screen and shield between man and his doom.

Benedictions on Muhammad, the Prophet of mercy and Chief of the Community, and on his family and Companions, the leaders of the truth and princes of the people – and many salutations.

* * *

The Pilgrimage is one of the pillars and fundamentals of Islam, the worship of a lifetime, the seal of consummation, the completion of surrender and the perfection of religion. It was during the Pilgrimage that God, Magnified and Glorious is He, sent down His revelation:

> 'Today I have perfected your religion for you, and completed My grace upon you, and approved Islam as your religion.' [al-Mā'idah, 5:3]
>
> (Al-yawma akmaltu lakum dinakum wa-atmamtu 'alaykum ni'matī wa-raḍītu lakumu-l'islāma dīnā.)

It was concerning the Pilgrimage that the Prophet, on him be peace, said: 'He who dies without having performed the Pilgrimage, let him die a Jew or a Christian, as he wishes.'[1]

Thus did he exalt an act of worship the omission of which deprives religion of its perfection, making one who forsakes it equal in error to a Jew or a Christian.

ITS EXCELLENCES AND ITS MERIT

The Excellent Merit of the Pilgrimage

God, Great and Glorious is He, said:

> 'And proclaim among men the Pilgrimage. They will come to you on foot and on every lean camel, coming from every deep ravine.' [al-Ḥajj, 22:27]
>
> (Wa-adhdhin fī-lnāsi bi-lḥajji ya'tūka rijālan wa-'alā kulli ḍāmirin ya'tīna min kulli fajjin 'amīq.)

Qatāda said that when God, Great and Glorious is He, commanded Abraham, on him be peace – and our Prophet and every chosen servant – to proclaim the Pilgrimage among men, he declared: 'O people! God, Great and Glorious is He, has built a House, so make Pilgrimage to it!'

The Exalted One said:

> 'That they may witness things beneficial to them.' [al-Ḥajj, 22:28]
>
> (Li-yashhadū manāfi'a lahum.)

When some referred this to trading at the season of Pilgrimage and reward in the Hereafter, one of the elders said: 'By the Lord of the Ka'ba, may they be forgiven!'

The words of God, Great and Glorious is He, in which Satan is made to say:

> 'I shall surely sit in ambush for them on Your straight path' [al-A'rāf, 7:16]
>
> (La-aq'udanna lahum ṣirāṭakumu-lmustaqīm.)

have been interpreted as meaning that Satan lurks on the road to Makka to keep people from getting there.

The Prophet, on him be peace, said: 'He who makes Pilgrimage to the House – avoiding indecent and immoral behaviour – emerges from his sins like a newborn babe.'[2] The Prophet, on him be peace, also said: 'Satan never appears smaller, more abject, more abased and more furious than on the day of 'Arafāt.'[3] This is simply because he sees mercy descending and sees God, Glorified is He, overlooking serious sins; for it is said that the only expiation for certain sins is standing at 'Arafāt. (Ja'far ibn Muhammad attributes this saying to God's Messenger, on him be peace.)[4]

One of those saintly people endowed with spiritual insight mentioned that Iblīs, on him be the curse of God, appeared to him at 'Arafāt in human form. He was thin, jaundiced, tearful and stooping. When asked the reason for his weeping, he said: 'The fact that the Pilgrims have set out towards God alone and not for doing business – I say, they have God alone as their destination. I fear they will not be thwarted, and that makes me unhappy.' He was then asked the cause of his thinness and he said: 'The neighing of the horses in the way of God, Great and Glorious is He. It would please me better if they were in my service.' The reason for his jaundiced complexion? 'The way they all assist each other in obedience. It would suit me better if they would help each other to disobey.' And what gave him that stoop? 'When a creature prays: "Grant me, I beseech You, a good conclusion," then I say: "Woe is me!" When he takes delight in his good work I am afraid he may have achieved sagacity.'

The Prophet, on him be peace, said: 'If someone sets out from his home as a Pilgrim or Visitant (*mu'tamir*) and then dies, he is granted the reward of a Pilgrim or Visitant till the Day of Resurrection. Anyone who dies in either of the Sanctuaries (Makka or Madina) is not subject to review or reckoning, but is told to enter Paradise.'[5]

And: 'A blessed Pilgrimage is better than this world and all it contains. For a blessed Pilgrimage there is no reward but Paradise.'[6]

Also: 'Pilgrims and Visitants are the emissaries and visitors of God, Great and Glorious is He; if they petition Him He gives what they ask, if they seek His forgiveness he forgives them, if they call on Him He answers, and if they seek intercession it is granted.'[7]

According to a Tradition handed down by the family of the Prophet, on them be peace: 'No-one sins more grievously than he who stands at 'Arafāt and supposes that God, Exalted is He, has not forgiven him.'[8]

According to Ibn 'Abbās, may God be pleased with him and his father, the Prophet, on him be peace, said: 'One hundred and twenty mercies descend upon this House each day: sixty for the circumambulants, forty for those performing Prayers and twenty for those who just look at it.'[9]

Another Tradition says: 'Make frequent circuits of the House, for this will be among the glories of your records on the Day of Resurrection, and the most fortunate action credited to you.'[10]

Circumambulation is therefore commendable on its own account, not only as part of the Pilgrimage or Visitation. Tradition tells us: 'To circuit seven times, barefoot or bareheaded, is as meritorious as freeing a slave, while he who circumambulates seven times in the rain is forgiven all his previous sins.'[11]

It is said that when God, Great and Glorious is He, forgives a sin for one servant at the place-of-standing (the plain of 'Arafāt), He forgives it for everyone there who is guilty of it. One of the elders said that when the Day of 'Arafāt coincides with the Day of Congregation (i.e. falls on a Friday), all those present at 'Arafāt are forgiven and it is the most excellent day in the world.

It was on such a day that God's Messenger, on him be peace, made his Farewell Pilgrimage.[12] While he was standing there he received the revelation from God, Great and Glorious is He:

> 'Today I have perfected your religion for you, and completed My grace upon you, and approved Islam as your religion.' [al-Mā'idah, 5:3]

The People of the Book said: 'If this revelation had come down to us, we would have made it a festival day.' Said 'Umar, may God be pleased with him: 'I am witness to the fact that it was on a double festival day that this revelation came down to God's Messenger as he was standing at 'Arafāt: the Day of 'Arafāt and the Day of Congregation.'

The Prophet, on him be peace, said: 'O God, forgive the Pilgrim and those for whom the Pilgrim seeks forgiveness!'[13]

It is related that 'Alī ibn Muwaffaq made several Pilgrimages on behalf of God's Messenger, on him be peace. He said: 'I then saw God's Messenger, on him be peace, in a dream, and he asked me: "Ibn Muwaffaq, did you make Pilgrimage on my behalf?" When I said yes, he said: "And you cried 'Labbayk' ('Doubly at Your service, Lord!') on my behalf?" I confirmed this and he said: "Then I shall reward you for it on the Day of Resurrection. I shall take you by the hand at the waiting place and lead you into Paradise, while all creatures are in dread of the reckoning."'

According to Mujāhid and other scholars, when the Pilgrims reach Makka they are met by the angels, who salute those riding camels, shake hands with those riding donkeys, and embrace those walking on foot. Al-Ḥasan says that anyone who dies just after Ramaḍān, just after a holy campaign or just after a Pilgrimage, dies a martyr. 'Umar said: 'The Pilgrim is forgiven, as are those for whom he seeks forgiveness in the months of Dhul Ḥijja, Muḥarram and Ṣafar, and twenty days of First Rabī'.'

It was the customary practice of the elders to see the warriors off on campaign and to greet the returning Pilgrims, kissing them between the eyes and asking for their Prayers; they did this promptly, before they had time to become sullied with sins.

'Alī ibn Muwaffaq is reported as saying: 'I made Pilgrimage one year and when the Night of 'Arāfat arrived I slept at Minā, in the Mosque of al-Khayf. There I dreamt that I saw two angels descending from heaven, clad in garments of green. One of them called out to his companion: "O servant of God!" and the other responded with "At your service, O servant of God!" The first then asked: "Do you know how many came on Pilgrimage this year to the House of God, Great and Glorious is He?" "No." "Six hundred thousand made the Pilgrimage to the House of our Lord. Do you know how many of them were accepted?" "No." "Only six souls." The two angels then rose into the air and disappeared from my view. At this point I awoke in dismay, feeling deep anxiety and concern. I said to myself: "If only six souls had their Pilgrimages accepted, where am I placed?" I then joined the stampede from 'Arafāt, stopping at Muzdalifa. I began to ponder how great was the multitude and how few would find acceptance, till sleep overtook me and I saw the two figures descending as before. They hailed each other, then one said: "Do you know what our Lord, Great and Glorious is He, has decreed tonight?" "No." "To each of the six he has given a hundred thousand." I awoke this time with a feeling of indescribable joy.'

He is further reported as saying, may God be pleased with him: 'I went on Pilgrimage one year, and after completing all the rites I thought about those whose Pilgrimages would not be accepted. Then I said: "O God, I donate my Pilgrimage and give the merit of it to someone whose Pilgrimage has not been accepted." I then dreamt of the Lord of might, Glorious is His majesty, Who said to me: "'Alī, you would be more generous than I, though it is I Who have created generosity and the generous! I, Who am the most Bounteous of the bountiful, the most Munificent of the munificent, more Worthy of bounty and generosity than the entire universe, I have bestowed all whose Pilgrimages I have not accepted upon those who have won My acceptance."'

Excellence of the Ka'ba and of Makka the Ennobled

The Prophet, on him be peace, said: 'God has promised this House that it will be visited every year by six hundred thousand Pilgrims. If they fall short of this number, God, Great and Glorious is He, makes it up from among the angels. The Ka'ba will be raised up at the Resurrection as if in a bridal procession; all who have made Pilgrimage to it will go around it, hanging on to its coverings, till it enters Paradise and they enter with it.'[14]

According to Tradition: 'The Black Stone is a ruby of Paradise. It will be raised on the Day of Resurrection with a pair of eyes and a tongue with which to speak, testifying for all who have touched it with truth and sincerity.'[15] The Prophet, on him be peace, used to kiss it often.[16] It is related that he, on him be peace, also prostrated himself upon it. If he rode on a camel, while circuiting around it, he touched it with a crooked staff and then kissed the end of the staff.[17]

'Umar, may God be pleased with him, kissed it, then said: 'I know you are a stone that neither harms nor helps, and had I not seen God's Messenger, on him be peace, kiss you, I would not have kissed you.' Then he wept, sobbing loudly. On turning round he saw 'Alī, may God ennoble his countenance and be pleased with him, and said: 'Here tears are shed and Prayers are answered, father of al-Ḥasan!' But 'Alī, may God be pleased with him, replied: 'Oh yes, Commander of the Believers, it does indeed harm and help!' 'How so?' 'When God, Exalted is He, took the Convenant from the descendants of Adam, He committed it to writing and embedded the document in this stone; it will therefore bear witness for the believer as to his fulfilment, and against the unbeliever as to his repudiation.'

This, they say, is the significance of the words people utter when touching the Black Stone:

> 'O God, I declare my belief in You, my acceptance of Your document and my fulfilment of Your covenant.'
>
> (Allāhumma īmānan bika wa-taṣdīqan bi-kitābika wa-wafā'an bi-'ahdika.)

Al-Ḥasan al-Baṣrī is reported as saying: 'One day of Fasting in Makka is worth a hundred thousand days, one penny in Alms is worth a thousand pounds, and any other good deed is likewise worth a hundred thousand times its value elsewhere.' It is said that to circumambulate seven times is equal to one Visitation, and that three Visitations are equal to one Pilgrimage. According to authentic Tradition: 'A Visitation in Ramaḍān is like performing a Pilgrimage with me'[18]

The Prophet, on him be peace, said: 'I shall be the first for whom the earth will split open, then I shall go to the cemetery called al-Baqī' (in Madina) and its occupants will be gathered up with me, then I shall go to the people of Makka and I shall be resurrected between the two Sanctuaries.'[19]

According to another Tradition: 'When Adam, on him be peace, had performed all the rites of Pilgrimage he was met by the angels, who said: "Blessed be your Pilgrimage, Adam. We made Pilgrimage to this House two thousand years before you did."'[20]

We have it from an early source that God, Great and Glorious is He, surveys the people of the earth every night; the first at whom He looks are the people of the Sanctuary (Makka), and of these He looks first at the people of the Sacred Mosque: those He sees circuiting He forgives, those He sees at Prayer He forgives, and those He sees standing facing the Ka'ba He forgives.

One of the saints, may God be pleased with them, saw a vision and said: 'I saw all the frontier regions prostrating toward 'Abbādān and I saw 'Abbādan prostrating towards Jidda.' It is said that the sun never sets on a day, nor rises after a night, when a saintly or holy person has not made the circuit of the House, and that when this ceases to be so there will be cause for the Ka'ba to be removed from the earth without trace. This will happen when nobody has come on Pilgrimage for seven years. The Quran will then be removed from the written books, leaving the pages blank with not one letter showing. Then the Quran will be erased from all hearts, not one word of it remembered. People will then revert to the poems, songs and fables of the time of Ignorance. Then will emerge the Antichrist and Jesus, on him be peace, will come down to kill him. The Hour of Resurrection will be at that moment as it were a pregnant woman on the verge of giving birth.

According to Tradition: 'Make frequent circumambulation of this House, before it is taken up; for twice it has been laid waste and the third time it will be taken away. '[21] It is related on the authority of 'Alī, may God be pleased with him, that the Prophet, on him be peace, said: 'God, Exalted is He, says: "If I wished to destroy the world I would begin by destroying My House, then I would destroy the whole world in its wake."'[22]

The Merit and Demerit of Residing in Makka,
may God, Exalted is He, protect her.

Cautiously apprehensive scholars find fault with permanent residence in Makka on three grounds:

One, fear of boredom and over-familiarity with the House, for this may tend to douse the ardour of reverence in the heart.

That was why 'Umar, may God be pleased with him, used to beat the people who had completed their Pilgrimage, crying: 'Yemenis, back to Yemen! Syrians, back to Syria! 'Irāqis, back to 'Irāq!' For the same reason 'Umar, may God be pleased with him, was careful to prevent people from excessive circumambulation, saying: 'I am afraid people will get too familiar with this House.'

Two, nostalgia stimulates a yearning to return. God, Exalted is He, has made the House a concourse secure for mankind, i.e. a place where they should congregate, returning to it time and again and never ceasing to aspire to it.

Someone said: 'That you should be in another town, with your heart yearning for Makka, attached to this House, is better for you than being there, bored with long residence and hankering after another town.' As one of the elders said: 'Many a man in Khurāsān is closer to this House than those circuiting around it!' It is even said that God, Exalted is He, has servants so close to Him, Great and Glorious is He, that the Ka'ba revolves around them.

Three, fear of committing errors and sins there. That is a grave peril, likely to excite the anger of God, Great and Glorious is He, on account of the nobility of the place.

Wuhayb ibn al-Ward, the Makkan, is reported as saying: 'One night as I was praying by the Black Stone, I heard a conversation between the Ka'ba and its coverings, in which it said: "To God I complain, and then to you, Gabriel, of what the circumambulants fling around me – the thoughts they give vent to, their vanities and their prattling. Unless they desist I shall surely give myself a mighty shake, sending every stone I am built with back to the hills from which they were hewn!"' Ibn Mas'ūd, may God be pleased with him, said: 'In no city but Makka is a man chastised for his mere intention, before he has acted on it.' Then he recited the words of the Exalted One:

> 'Whoever *purposes* to violate it wrongfully, We shall make him taste a painful doom.' [al-Ḥajj, 22:25]

[Wa-man yurid fīhi bi-ilḥādin bi-ẓulmin nudhiqhu min 'adhābin alīm.)

That is to say, punishment is entailed by the mere purpose.

It is said that evil deeds are compounded in Makka, as are good deeds. Ibn 'Abbās, may God be pleased with him, used to say: 'Monopolistic hoarding in Makka constitutes violation of the Sanctuary.' Some say the same of lying. Said Ibn 'Abbās: 'To sin seventy times at al-Rakīya would be preferable to me than to commit a single sin in Makka.'* Such fear has even led certain residents of Makka to make a practice of leaving the confines of the Sanctuary whenever they need to answer the call of nature. Someone stayed there a whole month without ever reclining on the ground. As a deterrent to long residence, certain scholars have expressed disapproval of renting houses in Makka.

Let it not be supposed that the demerit of residence is at odds with the merit of the place itself. The reason behind the former is human frailty and inability to treat the place with due respect. When we declare it preferable to forsake residing there, we refer to residence associated with inadequacy and boredom. As for its being preferable to residence in all propriety – how utterly absurd! Of course, for when God's Messenger, on him be peace, came back to Makka he approached the Ka'ba and said: 'You are the best spot on God's earth, Great and Glorious is He; most dear to me of all the cities of God, Exalted is He. If I had not had to leave you, I would never have left you.'[23] Of course, for it is an act of worship just to look upon the House, and good deeds performed there are compounded, as we have mentioned.

The Superiority of Madina the Radiant over Other Towns

After Makka itself, there is no place superior to Madina, the City of God's Messenger, on him be peace. Deeds performed there are also compounded. Said the Prophet, on him be peace: 'One Prayer in this Mosque of mine is better than a thousand Prayers in any other Mosque, except the Sacred

* al-Rakīya is a halt between Makka and al-Ṭā'if.

Mosque.'[24] Likewise every good action in Madina is worth a thousand. After the City of the Prophet comes the Holy Land of Jerusalem, where one Prayer is equal to five hundred elsewhere, with the exception of the Sacred Mosque. Again, the same is true of other deeds. Ibn 'Abbās relates that the Prophet, on him be peace, said: 'One Prayer in the Mosque of Madina is worth ten thousand Prayers, one Prayer in al-Aqṣā Mosque is worth a thousand, and one Prayer in the Sacred Mosque is worth a hundred thousand.'[25]

The Prophet, on him be peace, said: 'If anyone endures the rigours and austerity [of Madina], I shall be an intercessor for him on the Day of Resurrection.'[26] Also: 'If someone is able to die in Madina, let him die there, for no-one will die there without my being an intercessor for him on the Day of Resurrection.'[27]

Aside from these three places, all other districts are on an equal footing, with the exception of the frontier regions, where it is extremely meritorious to take up station. The Prophet, on him be peace, said: 'Only these three Mosques deserve a special journey: the Sacred Mosque, my Mosque and the Mosque of al-Aqṣā.'[28]

God's Messenger, on him be peace, also said: 'All countries are the countries of God, Exalted is He, so take up residence in any place where you find good company, and give praise to God, Exalted is He.'[29]

FINE POINTS OF PROPRIETY; INTERNAL CONDUCT

The fine points of propriety are ten in number:

PURITY OF INTENTION AND MEANS

1. The Pilgrim should meet his expenses by lawful *(Ḥalāl)* means and should have his hands free of any worrisome and distracting business concerns, so that his attention may be devoted exclusively to God, Exalted is He, and his heart directed in tranquillity to the remembrance of God, Exalted is He, and the veneration of His holy rites.

According to a Tradition handed down by relatives of the Prophet, on him be peace: 'At the end of the age, four classes of people will go on Pilgrimage: their rulers for the outing; their rich men for the trade; their poor men for the begging; their Quran-readers for the benefit of their reputations.'[30]

This indicates that all conceivable worldly purposes have some connection with the Pilgrimage. All of this negates the virtue of the Pilgrimage and depersonalises it, especially when the Pilgrimage itself is directly exploited by one who makes it on behalf of another in exchange for payment, seeking worldly gain by the work of the Hereafter. Pious and spiritual people disapprove of this, except where the intention of the person accepting payment is to settle in Makka and he lacks the means to get there; in that case there is no harm in it, the purpose being to use worldly means for religious ends and not vice-versa. In this instance his object must be to visit the House of God, Great and Glorious is He, while at the same time helping his Muslim brother by relieving him of his religious obligation. Relevant in this connection is the saying of God's Messenger, on him be peace: 'God, Glorified is He, admits three to Paradise for a single Pilgrimage: the testator who bequeaths it; the one who carries it out; and the one who performs it on behalf of his brother.'[31]

I am not saying that it is unlawful to make Pilgrimage on behalf of someone else, nor that one is forbidden to do so after having discharged one's personal obligation as a Muslim. It is better not to do so, however, and not to make it a livelihood and a business, for God, Great and Glorious is He, gives the world for religion, not religion for the world. According to the Tradition: 'He who goes on campaign in the cause of God, Great and Glorious is He, and takes a wage, is like the mother of Moses, on him be peace, who suckled her child and took her wage.'[32] He who takes hire for the Pilgrimage is similarly comparable to the mother of Moses; there is no harm in his doing so, for he takes it in order to have the possibility of making the Pilgrimage and visiting the Holy Places. He does not go on Pilgrimage to get the hire, but the other way round, just as Moses' mother accepted payment to facilitate her suckling by concealing her condition.

SHUNNING UNLAWFUL TAXES

2. The Pilgrim should not aid the enemies of God, Glorified is He, by paying tolls to those Makkan chiefs who bar the way to the Sacred Mosque, or Bedouin who lurk along the road. To pay these people is to encourage tyranny and to make it easy for them, for it is like giving them moral support. The Pilgrim should therefore devise some means of escape from such payment. If he is not capable of this, then according to some scholars (and it is not a bad opinion) it is better to turn back and abandon non-obligatory Pilgrimage rather than give assistance to tyrants, for this is an heretical innovation and acquiescence would tend to give it the force of custom. This form of taxation is degrading and humiliating to the Muslims.

There is no sense in saying: 'I had to pay up under duress.' If one had stayed at home or turned back one would not have had to pay a thing. Actually, a display of affluence sometimes provokes a lot of demands, whereas these would not arise if one dressed like the poor people; you may have only yourself to blame for putting yourself in a situation of duress.

MODERATION IN EXPENDITURE

3. Liberality in provision and magnanimity in outlay and expenditure, steering a middle course between stinginess and extravagance. I mean the lavish indulgence in exquisite food and drink, characteristic of the opulent. But heavy expense in giving generously is not extravagance, for there is no goodness in immoderation and no immoderation in goodness. Outlay on provision for the Pilgrimage is expenditure in the way of God,

Great and Glorious is He, and every penny of it is worth seven hundred. Said Ibn 'Umar, may God be pleased with him and with his father: 'Part of nobility consists in making generous provision for one's journey.' He also used to say: 'The most virtuous Pilgrim is he whose intention is most sincere, his expenditure most proper and his conviction most certain.'

The Prophet, on him be peace, said: 'For the Pilgrimage that is blessed there is no reward but Paradise.' When he was asked: 'O Messenger of God, what makes a Pilgrimage blessed?' he replied: 'Speaking well and feeding the poor.'[33]

FORSAKING EVIL CONDUCT

4. Forsaking indecency, immorality and wrangling, as spoken of in the Quran. Indecency is a general term, covering all nonsensical, foul and obscene language and including flirtation and dalliance with women as well as discussion of sexual intercourse and its preliminaries. Such talk excites the urge to unlawful intercourse, and incitement to what is forbidden is itself forbidden.

Immorality is another general term, covering all departures from obedience to God, Great and Glorious is He.

Wrangling is excessive quarrelling and argument, causing ill-will, distracting from noble purpose and incompatible with good character. As Sufyān said: 'Indecent behaviour vitiates one's Pilgrimage.' God's Messenger, on him be peace, set decent speech on a par with providing food as a cause of blessedness in the Pilgrimage, and quarrelling is incompatible with decent speech. One should therefore refrain from raising frequent objections against one's fellow traveller, the camels and one's other companions; rather should one take things gently, sheltering others beneath one's wing along the way to the House of God, Great and Glorious is He. Good conduct is essential, and good conduct means putting up with painful things rather than trying to repel them. They say that the Arabic word for 'journey' is *safar* because it reveals *(yusfiru 'an)* a person's character. That is why 'Umar, may God be pleased with him, asked someone who claimed to know a man: 'Have you accompanied him on a journey that would show up his good qualities?' Since the answer was no, he told him: 'Then I don't see how you can know him!'

GOING ON FOOT

5. Those who are able should make the Pilgrimage on foot, for this is the most meritorious way. At his death, 'Abdullāh ibn 'Abbās, may God be pleased with him and with his father, bequeathed this advice to his sons: 'My sons, go on foot when you make the Pilgrimage, because for every step the Pilgrim takes while walking he earns seven hundred of the bounties of the Sanctuary.' When asked what these bounties were, he replied: 'One good deed in the Sanctuary is rewarded a hundred thousand-fold.'

Walking between the various Hajj rituals, and when going to and fro between Makka, 'Arafāt and Minā, is even more strongly recommended than on the road to Makka. Going on foot, in conjunction with putting on the *Iḥrām* (entering the state of consecration) on leaving home, is said by some to constitute completion of Pilgrimage. Such was the construction put by 'Umar, 'Alī and Ibn Mas'ūd, may God be pleased with them, on the words of God, Great and Glorious is He:

> 'Complete the Pilgrimage and Visitation for God.' [al-Baqarah, 2:196]
>
> (Wa-atimmū-lḥajja wa-l'umrata lillāh.)

On the other hand, some scholars maintain that transport is better, in view of the outlay and provision involved and because it is less disturbing and painful and more conducive to a safe completion of the Pilgrimage.

This second opinion does not really contradict the first; one must consider which applies to a particular case. It is said that for one who can easily walk it is better that he do so, whereas transport would be preferable if he were weak, and if going on foot might affect him badly and restrict him in the performance of his duties. There is a parallel here with Fasting, which is better kept up even by the traveller and the invalid, unless it would cause weakness and bad temper.

A certain scholar was asked whether, in the Visitation (*'Umra*), one should go on foot or spend a little money on hiring a donkey. He replied that if one is more attached to the money, it is better to hire the donkey than to walk. But if walking is the more serious matter, as for the rich, then walking is to be preferred. There is something to be said for this view, which seems to make it a question of self-discipline. The best course of all, however, is to walk and spend the money on charity; this is superior to spending it on hiring a donkey. But for those who are incapable of giving up both personal comfort and their money, the opinion cited above is not inappropriate.

MODESTY AND SIMPLICITY OF TRANSPORT

6. The Pilgrim should take a simple riding-beast for transport, abstaining from being carried in a litter unless there is reason to fear that he could not ride the animal. There are two considerations here: (a) sparing the camel from the pain of bearing the litter; (b) avoiding an air of ostentatious luxury. God's Messenger, on him be peace, made the Pilgrimage on a riding camel, with a worn saddle and tattered pad, the cost of it being four dirhams.[34] He made circumambulation on the camel, so that people could observe his comportment and conduct.[35] The Prophet, on him be peace, said: 'Take your rituals from me.'[36]

They say these camel-litters were an innovation introduced by Pilgrims over the protests of the scholars of the day. Sufyān al-Thawrī reports his father as saying: 'En route from Kūfa to Qādisīya, bound for the Pilgrimage, I caught up with travelling companions from many lands. All the Pilgrims I saw had beasts of burden, animals carrying luggage, and riding-camels; among them all I spotted no more than two litters.' When Ibn 'Umar noticed the new styles and the litters introduced by the Pilgrims, he would say: 'Few Pilgrims, many riders!' Then he would look at a poor man, shabbily dressed and mounted atop some sacks, and say: 'This is the cream of the Pilgrims!'

SHABBINESS IN DRESS AND APPEARANCE

7. The Pilgrim should be shabbily dressed, dishevelled and dusty, not over-adorned nor inclined to things that excite vainglory and rivalry, thereby enrolling among the arrogant and the opulent and parting company with the weak, the poor and the righteous. For God's Messenger, on him be peace,

ordained dishevelment and inconspicuousness[37] and banned indulgence and luxury, according to the Tradition of Faḍāla ibn 'Ubayd.[38] As another Tradition puts it: 'The Pilgrim is nothing if not dishevelled and unkempt.'[39] According to yet another: 'God, Exalted is He, says: "Look at the visitors to My House; they come to Me, dishevelled and dusty, from every deep ravine."'[40] God, Exalted is He, said:

> 'Then let them finish their unkemptness . . .' [al-Ḥajj, 22:29]
>
> (Thumma la-yaqḍū tafathahum.)

'Unkemptness' means dishevelment and dustiness, and it is disposed of by shaving, trimming the moustache and clipping the nails. 'Umar ibn al-Khaṭṭāb, may God be pleased with him, wrote to the army commanders: 'Be smooth and be rough!' i.e. wear worn-out clothes and manage things roughly.

It has been said that the best Pilgrims are those from the Yemen, on account of their humble and gentle ways and because they follow the example set by the elders.

Red is to be avoided, especially in attire, as is commonplace notoriety. It is related that God's Messenger, on him be peace, was once on a journey when his Companions made a halt. As the camels were grazing, he noticed the red cloth on their humps. The Prophet, on him be peace, said: 'I see this colour red has got the better of you!'[41] Said the Companions: 'We therefore got up and removed the red cloth from their backs, until some of the camels bolted.'

KINDNESS TO BEASTS OF BURDEN

8. The Pilgrim must be kind to animals, taking care not to overload them. It is beyond their capacity to carry a litter, and sleeping in one imposes an intolerable weight. Pious people would not sleep on the back of an animal, unless they happened to doze off while riding. Nor would they stay mounted for long while the animal was kept standing. The Prophet, on him be peace, said: 'Don't treat the backs of your animals as chairs!'[42] It is recommended that one dismount both morning and evening to give one's beast a rest, following the Prophetic example and the precedents of the elders.[43]

One of the elders used to take an animal on hire with the stipulation that he would not dismount. Having paid the full price of hire, he would then get off the beast in order to do it a kindness, one that would be counted among his good deeds and weighed in his scale of the balance, not that of the owner.

Whoever harms a dumb creature and overloads it will be called to account for this on the Day of Resurrection. As he was dying, Abūl Dardā' said to a camel of his: 'Camel, do not complain of me to your Lord, for I have never overloaded you.'

In short, in every warm heart there lies a reward, so the right of the beast and the right of the hirer should both be respected; to dismount for a spell provides the animal with relief and pleases its hirer at the same time. A man once said to Ibn al-Mubārak: 'Carry this letter for me and deliver it.' But he replied: 'Let me first check with the camel-driver, for I have taken the animal on hire.' Note how cautious he was even about taking with him a virtually weightless letter! This is the prudent approach to piety, for once a door is ajar it gradually opens wider.

SACRIFICING ANIMALS

9. The Pilgrim ought to shed the blood of a sacrificial animal, even if it is not strictly incumbent upon him to do so, endeavouring to find a fine fat creature for the purpose. If the offering is voluntary he should eat some of it, but not if it is an obligatory sacrifice.* The words of God, Exalted is He:

> 'That . . . And whoever venerates God's consecrated offerings,' [al-Ḥajj, 22:32]
>
> (Dhālika wa-man yu'aẓẓim sha'ā'ira-llāh.)

have been interpreted as referring to the choice of a fine fat sacrificial animal.

It is preferable to drive the offering in from the assembly point, provided this is not too inconvenient and troublesome. One should refuse to pay sales-taxes, for three things get over-priced and reprehensibly taxed: offerings, sacrificial

---

* Some other opinions allow for eating from both.

slaughterings and slaves to be emancipated, since the best of these are the costliest and most precious to their owners.

According to Ibn 'Umar, 'Umar, may God be pleased with both father and son, was going to sacrifice a Bactrian camel. He was offered a price of three hundred dinars, so he asked God's Messenger, on him be peace, if he should sell it and use the money to buy several other animals, but he told him not to do that, saying: 'No, sacrifice it!'[44]

The reason for this is that a little of what is excellent is better than much that is inferior. Thirty beasts could have been purchased for the three hundred dinars, which would have represented a lot of meat. But the meat is not the object. The object is to purify the soul, to cleanse it of stinginess and to adorn it with the beauty of reverence for God, Great and Glorious is He, for:

> 'Their flesh and blood do not reach God, yet your devotion reaches Him.' [al-Ḥajj, 22:37]

This devotion is shown by regard for excellence of quality in the value, be the quantity great or small.

When God's Messenger, on him be peace, was asked what makes for a blessed Pilgrimage, he said: 'al-'ajj wa-lthajj (clamour and torrent).'[45] 'Clamour' refers to the loud voice used in calling: 'Labbayk' ('Doubly at Your service, Lord!'), while 'torrent' refers to the flow of blood at the slaughter of a sacrifice. 'Ā'isha, may God be pleased with her, relates that God's Messenger, on him be peace, said: 'No human action on the day of slaughter is dearer to God, Great and Glorious is He, than the shedding of blood, for it will come on the Day of Resurrection with its horns and its hooves; the blood will fall to some point at which God, Great and Glorious is He, will stop it reaching the ground. So rejoice with it!'[46]

According to another Tradition: 'There is a bounty for you in every hair of its hide, and every drop of its blood counts as a good deed to be weighed in the balance, so be of good cheer!'[47] The Prophet, on him be peace, said also: 'Seek the aid of your sacrificial offerings, for they will be your mounts on the Day of Resurrection.'[48]

EQUANIMITY

10. The Pilgrim should face with equanimity the expense he incurs to provision himself and acquire an offering, as well as any financial or physical loss or mishap that may befall him, for that is one of the signs that his Pilgrimage is accepted. Misfortune on the way to Pilgrimage is equated with expenditure in the cause of God, Great and Glorious is He, every penny being worth seven hundred. It is comparable to the rigours encountered en route to the Jihad, so for every hardship endured and for every loss suffered there is a recompense and nothing is lost in the sight of God, Great and Glorious is He.

One indication that a Pilgrimage has been accepted, they say, is when a Pilgrim abandons his sinful ways, exchanging his idle companions for righteous brothers, and forsaking haunts of frivolity and heedlessness in favour of gatherings for remembrance and vigilance.

INNER STATES AT VARIOUS STAGES OF HAJJ

The role of sincerity in intention. The way to respect the noble shrines, the manner in which to contemplate them and to reflect upon their mysteries and meanings, from the start of the Pilgrimage to the end.

The Pilgrimage begins with understanding, by which I mean the understanding of its place in the religion. The subsequent steps are then: yearning for it; resolving upon it; severing the ties that keep one from it; acquiring the seamless garments to be worn during consecration *(iḥrām);* purchasing the necessary provisions; hiring transport; setting out from home; crossing the desert; consecration at the assembly point, with the cry of 'Labbayk' ('Doubly at Your service, Lord!'); the entry into Makka; and then the completion of all the rites of Pilgrimage. Every one of these steps serves as a reminder to the mindful, a lesson to the heedful, an exhortation to the faithful aspirant, an instruction and indication to the sagacious. Let us therefore signify their key points, so that when the door to them is opened and their reasons known, some of their mysteries may be revealed to every Pilgrim, sufficient to afford him tranquillity of heart, inner purity and fullness of understanding.

UNDERSTANDING

As for understanding it must be realised that there is no way of attaining to God, Glorified and Exalted is He, except by divesting oneself of desires, abstaining from pleasures, confining oneself to necessities and devoting oneself exclusively to God, Glorified is He, in every movement and rest. It was for this reason that the ascetics of previous religions used to isolate themselves from the people, retiring to mountain caves and preferring solitude to the company of others, in quest of intimacy with God, Great and Glorious is He. For the sake of God, Great and Glorious is He, they forsook worldly pleasures and applied themselves to strenuous exertions in pursuit of the Hereafter. God, Great and Glorious is He, commends them in His Book, where He says:

'That is because among them there are priests and monks, and because they are not arrogant.' [al-Mā'idah, 5:82]

(Dhālika bi-anna minhum qissīsīna wa-ruhbānan wa-annahum lā yastakbirūn.)

But when all that had vanished, and people had become interested only in chasing their desires, shunning exclusive devotion to God, Great and Glorious is He, and getting lax about it, then God, Great and Glorious is He, sent His Messenger Muhammad, on him be peace, to revive the way of the Hereafter and to renew the method of travelling along it in accordance with the practice of God's Envoys.

Members of the earlier religious communities asked God's Messenger, on him be peace, if the ways of the monks and anchorites were followed in his religion and he replied: 'God has replaced them for us with the Jihad and the declaration of His supremacy on every elevated place.'[49] (Alluding to the Pilgrimage.) When asked about the anchorites, God's Messenger, on him be peace, said: 'They are the ones who Fast.'[50]

So God, Great and Glorious is He, has favoured this Community by making the Pilgrimage its form of monasticism and has honoured the Ka'ba, the Ancient House, by calling it His own, Exalted is He. He has made it a goal for His servants, consecrating its surroundings as a sanctuary for His House and for the glory of His cause. He has made 'Arafāt as it were the pipe supplying water to the pool of His heavenly court. He has emphasised the dignity of the place by declaring its game and its trees inviolate. He has modelled it on a royal durbar, the goal of visitors from every deep ravine and every distant scene, who come dishevelled, dusty and humble to the Lord of the House, meekly submissive to His majesty and might, (acknowledging, of course, that He is beyond being contained by any house or confined to any town) so that their homage and adoration may be more intense, their compliance and obedience more perfect. That is why they have been enjoined to perform there certain actions to which the soul does not readily conform, and the significance of which is not easily grasped by the mind, like the stoning of the pillars and the running back and forth several times between al-Ṣafā and al-Marwa. The Pilgrim demonstrates through such actions the perfection of his homage and adoration.

The Zakat has the rational appeal of an intelligible humane purpose. Fasting breaks the hold of desire, which is the tool of God's enemy, and is conducive to worship because it dispels distraction. Bowing and prostration in ritual Prayer promote humility toward God, Great and Glorious is He, through actions symbolic of humility, and the soul enjoys intimacy in the veneration of God, Great and Glorious is He. In actions like running to and fro or throwing pebbles, on the other hand, there is no pleasure or satisfaction and nothing to suggest any rational significance. The sole inducement to perform them is therefore the command itself and the intention to comply with it inasmuch as it is an order that must be obeyed.

Rationality is thus put aside, and the natural self is deflected from where its comfort lies; for if this was something readily comprehensible to the mind, there would be a natural inclination towards it. That inclination would then back up the command and provide an added incentive to act upon it, in which case it would hardly represent a perfect demonstration of homage and obedience. This is why God's Messenger, on him be peace, singled out the Pilgrimage when he said: 'Doubly at Your service, through a Pilgrimage in truth, devotion and homage!'[51] He did not say that about ritual Prayer or any other act of worship. If it were necessary to question the wisdom of God, Glorified and Exalted is He, in linking our salvation to actions that run counter to natural inclination and that are subject to the control of the Sacred Law, we would vacillate in the practice of obedience and following the dictates of submission. The performance of inexplicable duties is a form of devotion most effective in purifying the soul, and in deflecting it from its natural propensities into the habit of servitude. If you have grasped this, you will have understood that perplexity concerning these strange actions stems from inattention to the mysteries of devotions. This much will suffice, God willing, to impart an understanding of the essence of the Pilgrimage.

YEARNING

As for yearning: this arises only after understanding and the realisation that the House is truly the House of God, Great and Glorious is He, that it is modelled on the royal durbar so that he who goes there goes as a visitor to God, Great and Glorious is He, and that he who goes to the House in this world deserves that his visit should not be in vain. He will be accorded the object of his visit at the time appointed for him, namely the vision of God's Noble Countenance in the abode of eternity. For the inadequate mortal eye we possess in this earthly abode is unfitted to receive the vision of the Face of God, Great and Glorious is He, lacking the capacity to bear it or the equipment to take it in. But in the abode of the Hereafter, when it has been granted perpetuity and immunity to the causes of change and decay, it will be prepared for that vision and sight. Meanwhile, by betaking oneself to the House and beholding it, one earns the right to meet the Lord of the House in accordance with the noble promise.

To be sure, the yearning to meet with God, Great and Glorious is He, creates a longing for all that will lead to that meeting; for the lover craves everything in any way connected with his beloved. The House is connected with God, Great and Glorious is He, so this connection is surely enough in itself to make one yearn for it, quite apart from the wish to attain the abundant reward that is promised.

RESOLVE

As for resolve: the Pilgrim should be aware that by his resolve he is purposing to leave his family and homeland behind, forsaking pleasures and desires as he sets out to visit the House of God, Great and Glorious is He. He should hold in high esteem both the House and the Lord of the House. He must know that he has resolved upon a matter of high consequence and an affair of great moment. Where great things are at stake, the risks are also greatest. He should make sure his resolve is purely for the sake of God, Glorified is He, untarnished by hypocrisy and desire for fame. Let him be fully aware that only what is sincere in his intention and action will find acceptance, and that there is no offence more outrageous than to visit the House of God and His Sanctuary for ulterior motive. He should check with himself to verify his resolve: the verification is in his sincerity, and his sincerity lies in shunning all taint of hypocrisy and desire for fame. Let him therefore be careful to replace what is unworthy with something better.

SEVERING TIES

As for severing ties: this means the rejection of all iniquities and sincere repentance to God, Exalted is He, for all acts of disobedience, for each iniquity is a tie, and every tie is like having a creditor with you, clinging to your collar. He cries: 'Where are you heading for? Are you bound for the House of the King of kings, when you are neglecting His command here at home, belittling and ignoring it? Are you not ashamed to approach Him as a disobedient servant, since He will reject you and refuse you?' So if you hope to have your visit accepted you should carry out His commandments, cast off iniquities, repent to Him first of all for all acts of disobedience, and sever your heart's connection from concern with what is behind you. You can then turn your heart to face Him, as you turn your visible face in the direction of His House. Unless you do this, you will get nothing from your journey except trouble and hardship at the outset and dismissal and rejection at the end.

The Pilgrim should sever all ties with his homeland, cutting himself off completely as if he were going into exile, never to return. He should also write down his will and testament for his children and family, for the traveller and his money are at risk unless protected by God, Glorified is He.

While severing ties for the journey of Pilgrimage, one should also remember to be detached for the journey to the Hereafter, for that is soon to come. All that is suggested for this earthly journey is desirable in preparation for the other, which is to eternity and the ultimate return. One should therefore not be heedless of that final journey while getting ready for the Pilgrimage.

PROVISIONS

As for provisions: these must be acquired from a lawful source. If the Pilgrim feels himself impelled to take a lot, seeking enough to last him the whole journey without spoiling or going bad before he reaches his destination, let him remember that the journey to the Hereafter is a much longer one than this and that the provision for it is true piety. Apart from piety, whatever one supposes to be provision will be left behind when you die, leaving you in the lurch. It will no more keep than the fresh food that goes bad on the first leg of the journey, leaving one dismayed and helpless in the moment of need. Beware therefore, in case the deeds which make up your provision for the Hereafter do not go with you after death, but get spoiled instead by the taint of hypocrisy and the turbidity of remissness.

TRANSPORT

As for transport: when the Pilgrim procures a riding-beast, he should give heartfelt thanks to God, Great and Glorious is He, for putting animals at his disposal to relieve him of pain and hardship. At the same time he should call to mind the vehicle that will carry him to the abode of the Hereafter, namely his coffin, for the Pilgrimage presents a certain parallel to the final journey. He should therefore consider whether the journey he is about to make, riding this mount, will help to equip him for that other journey aboard that other vehicle. How close at hand it is! For all he knows, death may be so near that he will be riding the coffin before he has time to ride the camel. The coffin-ride is a certainty, whereas there is doubt about whether one can secure all one's needs for this trip. So where is the point in making careful preparations to equip oneself with provisions and transport for a doubtful journey, while neglecting the matter of one that is sure and certain?

PURCHASE OF IḤRĀM

As for the purchase of the two seamless garments of consecration: when buying his 'iḥrām' the Pilgrim should recall the shroud in which he will be wrapped for burial. When he nears the House of God, Great and Glorious is He, he will put on the two sheets, wearing one of them over one shoulder and the other as a sarong. While he may never finish his journey to the House of God, what is certain is that he must go to meet God, Great and Glorious is He, wrapped in the cloth of the shroud. He should therefore remember: just as he goes to meet the House of God, Great and Glorious is He, in unusual garb and attire, so after death he must go to meet God, Great and Glorious is He, dressed in a fashion different from that of this world. And the Pilgrim-garb is close to the other, being unstitched like the shroud.

LEAVING HOME

As for leaving home: the Pilgrim should know that he has now left hearth and home, bound for God, Great and Glorious is He, on a journey unlike any worldly voyage. He should be conscious in his heart of what he wishes, where he is heading and Whom he intends to visit. He should be aware that he is wending his way toward the King of kings, along with a host of visitors who have been summoned and have answered the call, in whom a great longing has been awakened, who have been roused and have risen, who have severed connections and said farewell to relations, and who have set out for the House of God, Great and Glorious is He, which is splendid in majesty and of lofty esteem. To encounter the House consoles them for not meeting its Lord, till they are granted their ultimate wish and rejoice in the contemplation of their Master.

The Pilgrim should also nourish in his heart the hope of attainment and of finding acceptance, not by virtue of his deeds in faring far from his family and property, but through trust in the bounty of God, Great and Glorious is He, and in hope of confirming His promise to those who visit His House.

He should nurture the hope that, if fate overtakes him en route and he does not arrive, he will meet God, Great and Glorious is He, coming to him, since He says (Glorious is His Majesty):

> 'Whoever sets out from his home, migrating to God and His Messenger, then death overtakes him, his recompense is incumbent upon God.' [al-Nisā', 4:100]
>
> (Wa-man yakhruj min baytihī muhājiran ilā-illāhi wa-rasūlihī thumma yudrikuhu-lmawtu faqad waqa'a ajruhū 'alā-llāh.)

CROSSING THE DESERT

As for crossing the desert to the assembly point, with all attendant hardships: the Pilgrim should there recall the crossing at death between this world and the assembly point on the Day of Resurrection, with the terrors and trials that intervene. The terror of highway robbers should remind him of the terror of the inquisition by Munkar and Nakīr;* the savage beasts of the desert should make him think of the scorpions and worms of the tomb, with its vipers and serpents; his separation from family and relatives should put him in mind of the desolation of the tomb, of its agony and solitude. Through all these terrors he should equip himself by word and deed for the horrors of the tomb.

PUTTING ON IḤRĀM AND CRYING 'LABBAYK'

As for donning the garb of consecration and crying 'Labbayk' from the assembly point onwards: the Pilgrim should know that this signifies a response to the summons of God, Great and Glorious is He. Hope, therefore, to be accepted and dread being told: 'No favour or fortune for you!' Oscillate between hope and fear; rid yourself of your power and strength, and rely on the grace and generosity of God, Great and Glorious is He. The moment of *talbiya* (calling 'Labbayk') is the real starting point – this is the critical instant. Sufyān ibn 'Uyayna said: "Alī, the son of al-Ḥusayn,may God be pleased with them both, once went on Pilgrimage. When he had put on his *iḥrām* and his camel was ready for him to ride, he suddenly turned pale and began to tremble. He shivered and quaked and could not utter "Labbayk", and when they asked him what was wrong he said: "I dread being told: 'No favour or fortune for you!'" When he did eventually cry "Labbayk", he fainted and fell from his camel. This kept on happening to him until he had completed his Pilgrimage.'

Aḥmad ibn Abīl Ḥawārī said: 'I was with Abū Sulaymān al-Dārānī, may God be pleased with him, when he wished to enter the state of consecration. He did not utter "Labbayk" until we had travelled a whole mile. He fell in a swoon, saying when he came to: "Ahmad! God, Glorified is He, inspired to

---

* Two angels who will question the dead in his grave.

Moses, on him be peace: 'Tell the wrongdoers among the Children of Israel to remember Me seldom, for I shall remember with a curse those of them who remember Me.' Alas, Ahmad, I have heard that to those who make Pilgrimage on ill-gotten gains, God, Great and Glorious is He, says: 'No favour or fortune for you, until you return what you have in hand.' And we cannot be sure that this will not be said to us."'

On raising his voice at the assembly point with the cry of 'Labbayk', the Pilgrim should recall that he is responding to the summons of God, Great and Glorious is He, since He said:

> 'And proclaim the Pilgrimage among men.' [al-Ḥajj, 22:27]
> (Wa-adhdhin fī-lnāsi bi-lḥajj.)

He should also recall that mankind will be summoned by the trumpet's blast, gathered up from the tomb and crowded together at the site of the Resurrection, responding to the call of God, Glorified is He, divided into the favoured and the abhorred, the accepted and the rejected, and oscillating initially between fear and hope – like the Pilgrims at the assembly point, when they do not know whether or not they will be enabled to complete the Pilgrimage and have it accepted.

ENTERING MAKKA

As for entering Makka: The Pilgrim should remember at this time that he has arrived safely at the Sanctuary of God, Exalted is He. As he enters he should hope to be safe from the punishment of God, Great and Glorious is He, and should dread not being worthy to approach Him, for in that case his entry into the Sanctuary would leave him frustrated and fit to be abhorred. At all times his hope should be uppermost, for God's generosity is comprehensive, the Lord is Compassionate, the honour of the House is tremendous, the visitor's right is respected, and protection is secure for all who seek refuge.

SEEING THE KA'BA

As for setting eyes upon the House: at this moment the Pilgrim should be conscious in his heart of the majesty of the

House, venerating it with such intensity that he seems to anticipate beholding the Lord of the House. He should hope that God, Exalted is He, will grant him the vision of His noble countenance, just as He has afforded him the sight of His mighty House. Thank God, Great and Glorious is He, for bringing you to this high degree, and for including you in the company of those who reach Him. Remember at the same time how at the Resurrection people will stream towards Paradise, all hoping to enter there, and how they will be divided into those who are admitted and those who are turned away, just as the Pilgrims are divided into the accepted and the rejected. In all that you see, take care to recall the things of the Hereafter, for every aspect of the Pilgrimage reflects some aspect of the Hereafter.

CIRCUMAMBULATING THE HOUSE (ṬAWĀF)

As for the circumambulation of the House: realise that it is a ritual Prayer. While making it, you should fill your heart with reverence, fear, hope and love. Know that in your circuit you resemble the angels near the Divine presence, who ring the Throne and circle around it. Do not suppose the purpose to be your bodily circumambulation of the House. No, the true purpose is the circling by your heart in remembrance of the Lord of the House, till remembering begins with Him alone and ends with Him alone, just as the circumambulation starts from the House and ends at the House. Know that the noble circumambulation is the circling by the heart in the Divine presence, and that the House is the external symbol in the visible world for the unseen Divine court which lies in the invisible universe. For those to whom God opens the door, the material and visible world is but the threshold of the invisible, angelic universe. This parallel is suggested by the correspondence between the Populous House *(al-bayt al-ma'mūr)* in heaven and the Ka'ba.

The heavenly circling of the angels is like the human circumambulation of this House, but since most people are incapable of achieving that level of circumambulation, they have been commanded to imitate as best they can, with the promise that: 'He who imitates a set of people is one of them.'[52] Of those who are capable of that kind of circumambulation, it is said that the Ka'ba visits them and makes circuit around them; visionaries have seen this happen to certain intimates of God, Glorified and Exalted is He.

TOUCHING THE BLACK STONE

As for touching the Black Stone: believe when you do this that you are swearing allegiance to God, Great and Glorious is He, and vowing obedience to Him. Make firm your resolve to be loyal to your oath, for the wrath of God is the traitor's due. Ibn 'Abbās, may God be pleased with him and his father, relates that God's Messenger said: 'The Black Stone is the right hand of God, Great and Glorious is He, on earth; with it he shakes hands with His creatures, just as a man shakes hands with his brother.'[53]

STANDING AT MULTAZAM

As for clinging to the coverings of the Ka'ba, and pressing one's breast against its wall (at the part called *al-multazam):* your intention in the latter should be to draw close in love and yearning to the House and the Lord of the House, seeking grace through the contact and hoping for immunity from the Fire, not in the House but in every part of your body. In clinging to the coverings of the Ka'ba, your intention should be earnestly to seek forgiveness and to beg for mercy, just as one who has sinned against another will cling to his clothes while imploring his pardon, demonstrating that he has no refuge or recourse except to his munificence and forgiveness and that he will not let go until he is granted pardon and the assurance of future protection.

RUNNING BETWEEN AL-ṢAFĀ AND AL-MARWA (SA'Y)

As for running between al-Ṣafā and al-Marwa in the courtyard of the House: this resembles the constant to-ing and fro-ing of a servant in a royal palace. The Pilgrim demonstrates devotion to duty and hopes to be viewed with compassion, just like one who enters the presence of a king and leaves without knowing whether the sovereign has decided to accept or to reject him. He keeps going back across the courtyard time after time, hoping to receive mercy the second time if not the first. While going back and forth between al-Ṣafā and al-Marwa, the Pilgrim should recall how he will oscillate between the two scales of the Balance at the site of the Resurrection. He should let al-Ṣafā represent the scale of good deeds and al-Marwa the scale of bad deeds. Let him recall how he shall go from one of these to the other, seeing which is heavier or lighter, fluctuating between punishment and forgiveness.

STANDING AT 'ARAFĀT

As for standing at 'Arafāt: recall – when you behold the thronging crowds, hear the loud voices speaking in many tongues, and see the various groups following their Imams through the ritual observances, matching their actions to theirs – recall the site of the Resurrection, the gathering of the communities with their Prophets and leaders, each community following its Prophet, aspiring after his intercession, all wavering with equal uncertainty between rejection and acceptance. After that recollection, set your heart on supplication and entreaty to God, Great and Glorious is He, that you may be resurrected in the company of the mercifully successful; make certain your hope of being answered, for the place is noble and mercy reaches all creatures from the majesty of the Divine presence through the venerable hearts of the mainstays of the earth. The standing-place is never devoid of a generation of the saintly and holy, nor of a generation of the righteous and magnanimous. When their aspirations are joined, their hearts devoted exclusively to humble supplication and entreaty, their hands raised to God, Glorified is He, their necks outstretched and their eyes turned heavenward, as they aspire of one accord in quest of mercy, do not suppose that He will disappoint their hopes, frustrate their endeavour or begrudge them an overwhelming mercy. That is why it is said that it is a most grievous sin to be present at 'Arafāt and to imagine that God, Exalted is He, does not forgive one. It would seem that the conjunction of aspirations, and the strength derived from contiguity with the saintly and holy people assembled from all quarters of the earth, constitute the secret of the Pilgrimage and its ultimate purpose, for there is no way to obtain the mercy of God, Glorified is He, in such abundance as by the conjunction of aspiration and the simultaneous mutual support of all hearts.

CASTING PEBBLES (RAMY)

As for the casting of pebbles (at pillars representing the Devil): your purpose in this should be obedience to the Divine command, to demonstrate submissiveness and servitude and readiness to comply without any obvious rational or psychological justification.

It should also be one's intention to imitate Abraham, on him be peace, since it was in this place that Iblīs, on him be the curse of God, Exalted is He, appeared to him to insinuate doubt about his Pilgrimage or to tempt him to disobey, whereupon God, Great and Glorious is He, commanded him to throw stones at him to repel him and thwart his design. If it should occur to you to think: 'Satan appeared to him and he actually saw him – that was why he stoned him – but the Devil is not showing himself to me,' you must realise that this very notion comes from the Devil; it is he who has lodged it in your heart, to weaken your determination in casting the stones, to make you imagine that it is a useless action, like some kind of game, so why should you bother with it? Therefore you must drive him from your soul by being earnest and brisk in stoning him, putting the Devil's nose out of joint.

You should be aware that, while outwardly casting pebbles at the pillar, you are really throwing them in the face of Satan and dealing him a mortal blow, for the only way to spite him is through your compliance with the command of God, Glorious and Exalted is He, in simple deference to His order without psychological or intellectual justification.

SACRIFICING ANIMALS

As for the slaughter of the sacrificial offering: be aware that this is a means of drawing close to God, Exalted is He, by virtue of obedience, so make the sacrifice perfect and hope that for every part of it God will deliver part of you from the Fire. A promise to this effect has come down to us.[54] The bigger the sacrificial animal and the more ample its parts, therefore, the more comprehensive your redemption from the Fire.

VISITING MADINA

As for the visit to Madina: when your eyes alight on the city walls, remember that this is the town which God, Great and Glorious is He, selected for His Prophet, on him be peace, that he made it the goal of his migration, that this was his home where he promulgated the binding decrees of his Lord, Great and Glorious is He, established his own exemplary precedents, strove against his foes and proclaimed his religion until God, Great and Glorious is He, took him to Himself. It then came to house his tomb, and the tombs of two of his aides who upheld the truth after him, may God be pleased with them.

Envisage, next, the footprints of God's Messenger, on him be peace, as he went about the city. Aware that his precious feet have trodden in every place where feet may tread, you must walk with dignity and caution. Recall how he used to walk about its streets, picturing to yourself his humility and his graceful gait. Think of the tremendous wisdom God, Glorified is He, entrusted to his heart, how He has exalted his memory along with His own, Exalted is He, even linking remembrance of him to remembrance of Himself,* and how He frustrated the work of those who showed him disrespect, if only by raising their voices above his. Reflect then on the great favour God, Exalted is He, bestowed on those who enjoyed his fellowship, and who were so fortunate as to see him in the flesh and to hear him speak. You should feel a great regret at having missed his companionship, and that of his Companions, may God be pleased with them. Go on to recall how you have missed seeing him in the Hereafter. Perhaps you will see him, but only in remorse, prevented from being accepted by him because of your evil conduct, for as he said, on him be peace: 'God will raise certain people to me and they will say: "O Muhammad!" I shall say: "Lord, these are my Companions." But He will say: "You do not know what practices they introduced after you had left them." Then I shall say: "Let them be far removed from me!"'[55]

---

* In the affirmation of faith: 'There is none worthy of worship but God, and Muhammad is the Messenger of God.'

If you have ceased to respect his Sacred Law, be it only for one instant, you have no guarantee that you will not be debarred from him because of your deviation from his way. Great should be your hope, nonetheless, that God, Exalted is He, will not keep you from him after He has granted you faith and sent you forth from your homeland in order to visit him, not for purposes of trade or worldly gain, but purely from love of him and longing to behold his relics and the wall of his tomb. Since you embarked on this journey for that reason alone, having missed the opportunity of seeing him in the flesh, you surely deserve the compassionate regard of God, Exalted is He.

On reaching the Mosque, you should recall that this is the site selected by God, Glorified is He, for His Prophet, on him be peace, and for the first and most virtuous of the Muslims. Remember that the laws decreed by God, Glorified is He, were first observed at this spot, and that the best of God's creatures, living or dead, have gathered here. Be most hopeful, therefore, that God, Glorified is He, will mercifully bless your entrance, and make that entrance in all humility and veneration. How worthy is this place to inspire humility in the heart of every believer! As Abū Sulaymān is reported to have said: 'Uways al-Qaranī, may God be pleased with him, went on Pilgrimage and entered Madina. When he stood at the gate of the Mosque he was told: "This is the tomb of the Prophet, on him be peace." He fell in a faint, and when he revived he said: "Send me away, for I cannot enjoy myself in a town where Muhammad, on him be peace, lies buried!"'

VISITING GOD'S MESSENGER

As for visiting God's Messenger, on him be peace: you must stand before him in the manner we have described, visiting him in death as you would have visited him in life. Do not approach his tomb except as you would have approached his noble person if he had been alive. Just as you would have considered it respectful to refrain from touching or kissing his person, rather standing back and bowing before him, you should now act accordingly. Touching and kissing tombs is a custom of Christians and Jews. Realise that he is aware of your presence, of your standing there and of your visit; that he is receiving your greeting and benediction. Imagine his noble form as it lies in the tomb in front of you. Feel in your heart his tremendous dignity. For he is reported as saying that God, Exalted is He, has appointed to his tomb an angel who conveys to him the salutations of those members of his Community who salute him.[56]

This refers to those who are not actually present, so how about those who leave home and cross desert wastes from longing to meet him, content merely to behold his noble shrine since they have no possibility of witnessing his noble countenance? He said, on him be peace: 'When someone blesses me once, God blesses him ten times.'[57] This refers to the reward for oral benediction, so how about the reward for coming in person to visit him?

Next, you should go to the pulpit of God's Messenger, on him be peace, imagining you can see the Prophet, on him be peace, ascending it. Picture to yourself his radiant appearance, as if he were there on the pulpit, surrounded by the Emigrants and Helpers, may God be pleased with them, as he urges them in his sermon to be obedient to God, Great and Glorious is He. Ask God, Great and Glorious is He, not to part you from him at the Resurrection.

Conclusions

Such are the duties of the heart at all stages of the Pilgrimage. When all have been completed, your heart should be beset with sadness, anxiety and fear, for you do not know whether you have had your Pilgrimage accepted and been firmly placed in the company of the loved ones, or had your Pilgrimage rejected and been included among the outcasts. The Pilgrim should discover this from his heart and its conduct. If he finds his heart extremely adverse to this world of delusion and inclined to that of intimacy with God, Exalted is He, and if he finds its conduct to have been weighed with the balance of the Sacred Law, then he may count on acceptance, for God, Exalted is He, accepts only those He loves. To those He loves He extends His care and the marks of His affection, guarding them from the onslaught of His enemy Iblīs, on him be the curse of God. If these signs are apparent, they point to accept-

5
The Night Vigil

QIYĀM AL-LAYL

QURANIC VERSES

The pertinent Qur'ānic Verses are these words of God, Glorified and Exalted is He:

> 'Your Lord knows that you keep vigil nearly two-thirds of the night, or half or one-third of it, as do a group of those with you . . .' [al-Muzzammil, 73:20]
>
> 'The first part of the night is indeed the time when impressions are strongest and speech most direct.' [al-Muzzammil, 73:6]
>
> 'Their sides forsake their couches as they call on their Lord in fear and hope . . .' [al-Sajdah, 32:16]
>
> 'Is he who devotes the night-hours to worship, prostrating himself and standing up in Prayer, aware of the Hereafter and hoping for the mercy of his Lord . . .?' [al-Zumar, 39:9]
>
> 'And who spend the night before their Lord, prostrating themselves and standing up . . .' [al-Furqān, 25:64]
>
> 'Look for help in patience and Prayer* . . .' [al-Baqarah, 2:45]

TRADITIONS OF THE PROPHET

Relevant Traditions include the following sayings of the Prophet, on him be peace:

---

* Some say this refers to the night vigil, when the aid of patience must be sought in the struggle with the tower self.

'While any one of you is sleeping, Satan ties three knots on the nape of your neck, and all night long he strikes the spot where each knot is tied, keeping you asleep. But if you wake up and remember God, Exalted is He, one knot is undone; if you perform the ritual ablution, a second knot is untied; if you perform the Prayer, the third knot is loosened and in the morning you will be fresh and in good spirits – otherwise the morning will find you bad-tempered and slothful.'[1]

(On hearing about a man who used to sleep all night right through till morning): 'Satan has urinated in that man's ear.'[2]

'Satan has a kind of snuff, a kind of syrup and a kind of powder. When he gets a man to take this snuff, the man becomes badly behaved; when he administers the syrup, the man becomes sharp- and evil-tongued; when he applies the powder, the man sleeps right through the night till morning.'[3]

'Two cycles of Prayer performed in the middle of the night are better for a man than the world and all it contains. But for the hardship it would have caused my Community, I would have made them compulsory.'[4]

'There is an hour of the night when, if any Muslim asks God, Exalted is He, for something good, He is sure to grant it to him.' Or, in another version: '. . . asks God, Exalted is He, for something good of this world or the Hereafter. And that is every night.'[5]

According to Mughīra ibn Sha'ba, God's Messenger, on him be peace, would get up to pray until his feet were splitting. Someone said to him: 'Surely God has forgiven you your former and your latter sins?' But he replied: 'Should I not be a grateful servant?'[6] What is clearly implicit here is an allusion to increase in stature, for gratitude is the cause of augmentation. In the words of God, Exalted is He:

> 'If you give thanks, I will surely give you more.' [Ibrāhīm, 14:7]
>
> (La-in shakartum la-azīdannakum.)

The Prophet, on him be peace, said: 'Abū Hurayra, do you wish to enjoy God's mercy in life and in death, in the tomb and at the Resurrection? Then get up at night and pray! Do you wish for your Lord's approval, Abū Hurayra? Then pray in the corners of your house; your house will be as radiant in heaven as the light of the planets and stars is to people on earth.'[7]

The Prophet, on him be peace, also said: 'It is incumbent upon you to observe night vigil, for it was the practice of your righteous predecessors. Night vigil brings us close to God, Great and Glorious is He, atones for our sins, drives disease from the body and puts a stop to transgression.'[8]

The Prophet, on him be peace, said: 'Whenever a man is overtaken by sleep while performing Prayer at night, the reward for his Prayer is recorded in his favour and his sleep is reckoned as Alms.'[9]

God's Messenger, on him be peace, said to Abū Dharr: 'If I were intending to make a journey, would I get provisions ready for it?' 'Yes,' said he. 'Well, Abū Dharr, how about the journey on the way to the Hereafter? Shall I not tell you what will be useful to you on that day?' 'Of course! You are more to me than my father and mother.' 'Fast on a very hot day, in preparation for the Day of Resurrection; perform two Prayer-cycles in the darkness of night, in readiness for the desolation of the tomb; make a Pilgrimage, for portentous events; do an act of charity, by giving Alms to a pauper, by speaking a word of truth, or by holding back a word of evil.'[10]

It is related that in the time of the Prophet, on him be peace, there was a man who, when others took to their beds and closed their eyes, would get up to pray and recite the Quran, saying: 'Lord of the Fire, deliver me from it.' When this was mentioned to the Prophet, on him be peace, he said: 'Notify me when this happens.' Then he came to him and he heard for himself. When morning came he said to him: 'So-and-so, have you not asked God for Paradise?' But he replied: 'Messenger of God, I am not there, nor do my deeds amount to that.' Shortly after this, Gabriel, on him be peace, descended and said: 'Tell so-and-so that God has already delivered him from the Fire and admitted him to Paradise.'[11]

It is further related that Gabriel, on him be peace, said: 'Ibn 'Umar would be such a good man if only he would pray at night!' The Prophet, on him be peace, informed him of this and from then on he always kept night vigil.[12]

Nāfi' said: 'Ibn 'Umar would pray through the night, then say: "Nāfi', is it time for the pre-dawn meal?" When I said "No," he would resume his Prayers. Then he would ask me again, and when I said: "Yes," he would sit down and beg forgiveness of God, Exalted is He, till the dawn broke.'

Said 'Alī ibn Abī Ṭālib: 'Yaḥyā, the son of Zakariyā, on both of them be peace, ate his fill of barley and went to sleep without reciting his devotions. When morning came, God, Exalted is He, said to him by inspiration: "Yaḥyā, have you found a dwelling better for you than My dwelling? Or have you found a neighbourhood better for you than My neighbourhood? By My might and majesty, Yaḥyā, if you took one look at Paradise your fat would melt and your soul would expire from yearning, while if you took one look at Hell your fat would melt, you would weep pus after tears and wear leather after haircloth."'

God's Messenger, on him be peace, was told: 'So-and-so prays during the night and in the morning he steals.' Said he: 'His good action will cause him to desist.'[13]

The Prophet, on him be peace, said: 'God grants His mercy to a man who gets up in the night to pray, then wakes up his wife to pray also, sprinkling water on her face if she is unwilling.'[14] He also said, on him be peace: 'God grants His mercy to a wife who gets up in the night to pray, then rouses her husband to pray also, sprinkling water on his face if he is unwilling.'[15] Further: 'If a man wakes up at night and rouses his wife, and they both perform two cycles of Prayer, they are recorded among the men and women who remember God very often.'[16]

The Prophet, on him be peace, also said: 'The best Prayer after the (five) prescribed is the night vigil.'[17]

Said 'Umar ibn al-Khaṭṭāb, may God be pleased with him: 'The Prophet, on him be peace, said: "If someone misses his portion of Quran-recitation, or part of it, through sleeping at night, then makes up his reading between the dawn- and midday-Prayers, it will be recorded in his favour as if he had done his reading at night."'[18]

TRADITIONS OF THE COMPANIONS AND THEIR FOLLOWERS

Among the Traditions of the Companions, it is related that 'Umar, may God be pleased with him, would be going over the Verse from his nightly recitation till he fainted and dropped, so then he would be visited because of this for several days as a sick man receives visits. When others' eyes were asleep, Ibn Mas'ūd, may God be pleased with him, would get up and until morning a droning sound could be heard from him like the droning of bees. It is said that Sufyān al-Thawrī, may God grant him His mercy, ate his fill one night, saying: 'When the donkey gets extra fodder, it works all the harder.' Then he kept vigil that night through till morning. When Ṭā'ūs, may God grant him His mercy, reclined on his bed he would feel as restless as peas in a frying-pan, so he would jump up and pray till morning. Then he would say: 'The recollection of Hell sends the sleep of the worshipful flying!'

Said al-Ḥasan, may God grant him His mercy: 'We know of no harder act of piety than enduring through the night and offering up our money.' He was asked: 'How is it that those who observe the Prayers of night vigil are among the people with the most beautiful faces?' To this he replied: 'Because they commune with the All-merciful and He clothes them in light from His light.'

A certain righteous man came home from his travels. His bed was laid out for him and he fell asleep on it, missing his recitations. He swore that never again would he sleep on a bed. 'Abd al-'Azīz ibn Rawwād used to go to his bed when night had fallen, saying as he stroked it with his hand: 'You are soft indeed, but by God there is in Paradise a softer one than you!' Then he would spend the whole night in Prayer. Said al-Fuḍayl: 'I approach the night at the outset and the length of it appals me; then I start on the Quran and it is already morning before I have satisfied my craving.'

Said al-Ḥasan: 'A man commits a sin and because of it he is deprived of night vigil.' Al-Fuḍayl said: 'If you are incapable of keeping night vigil and of Fasting by day, you must know that you are under interdiction because of your many faults.' Ṣila ibn Ashyam, may God grant him His mercy, used to pray throughout the night. Shortly before dawn he would say: 'My God, it is not for the likes of me to ask for Paradise, but deliver me by Your mercy from the Fire!' A man said to one of the wise: 'I am really too weak to keep night vigil.' So the wise man told him: 'My brother, do not disobey God, Exalted is He, and you need not stay up at night.'

Al-Ḥasan ibn Ṣāliḥ had a slave-girl, whom he sold to some people. This slave-girl got up in the middle of the night, crying: 'People of the house, Prayers, Prayers!' They said: 'Is it morning already? Has the dawn broken?' Said she: 'Do you mean to say you only observe the five set Prayers?' When they said yes, she went back to al-Ḥasan, saying: 'Master, would you sell me to people who only observe the set Prayers? Take me back!' So he took her back.

Said al-Rabī': I spent many nights in the house of al-Shāfi'ī, may God be pleased with him, and he never slept more than a very short part of the night.' Abūl Juwayrīya said: 'I kept company with Abū Ḥanīfa, may God be pleased with him, for six months and there was not one night in all that time when he laid his side on the ground.' Abū Ḥanīfa used to stay awake half the night, but as he was passing some people he heard them say: 'This man stays awake the whole night,' so he retorted: 'I am ashamed to be credited with something I do not do.' From then on he took to staying awake all night long. It is related too that he had no bedding for the night.

They say that Mālik ibn Dīnār, may God be pleased with him, spent the whole night through till morning repeating this Verse:

> 'Or do those who commit bad deeds suppose that We shall make them like those who believe and do good works . . .' [al-Jāthiyah, 45:21]
>
> (Am ḥasiba-lladhīna-jtaraḥū-lsayyi'āti an naj'alahum ka-lladhīna āmanū wa-'amilū-lṣāliḥāt.)

Said al-Mughīra ibn Ḥabīb: 'I noticed Mālik ibn Dīnār performing ablution after the late evening Prayer, then he went and stood at his place of Prayer. He took hold of his beard, and choking with tears, began to say: "My God, preserve Mālik's grey hairs from the Fire! You know the inhabitant of Paradise from the inhabitant of Hell-fire, so which of the two is Malik?" He went on saying this till break of day. Mālik ibn Dīnār also said: "One night I went to sleep, forgetting my recitations. In my dreams I found myself with a most beautiful girl. In her hand she held a piece of paper and asked me: 'Can you read well?' When I told her I could, she handed me the paper, on which these lines were written:

Have pleasures and desires distracted you
from Paradise with maidens fair and sweet?
There you shall dwell eternally and sport
with all the lovely ladies you shall meet.
From dreams awake and – better far than sleep –
recite Quran until the dawn you greet."'

It is said that when Masrūq went on Pilgrimage he spent every night prostrating himself in worship. And it is related on the authority of Azhar ibn Mughīth (one of those devoted to constant Prayer) that he said: 'I dreamt I saw a woman unlike earthly women, so I said to her: "Who are you?" and she replied: "One of the maidens of Paradise." I then asked her to marry me and she said: "Put your proposal to my master, and pay me my dower." "And what is your dower?" I asked. "Long Prayers of night vigil," she replied.'

Yūsuf ibn Mihrān said: 'I have heard that beneath the Throne there is an angel in the shape of a cock. Its talons are of pearl and its spurs of green topaz. When the first third of the night has passed it flaps its wings, crows and says: "Let those who get up arise!" When half the night is gone by it again flaps its wings, crows and says: "Let those who keep vigil arise!" Then when two-thirds of the night have passed it once more flaps its wings, crows and says: "Let those who pray arise!" Finally, when dawn breaks it flaps its wings, crows and says: "Let the heedless arise, bearing the weight of their sins!"'

They say that Wahb ibn Munabbih al-Yamānī never laid his side on the ground in thirty years, and that he used to say: 'I would rather see a devil in my house than a pillow, for that is an invitation to sleep.' He had a leather cushion, on which he would place his breast when sleep overpowered him. After nodding a few times he would then make haste to pray.

Someone said: 'I saw the Lord of Glory in a dream and heard Him say: "By My Glory and Majesty, I shall surely honour the abode of Sulaymān al-Taymī, for he has prayed to me each morning for forty years without breaking his ablution made for late evening prayer."' He is said to have held the view that when sleep penetrates the heart it invalidates the ritual ablution.

In one of the ancient scriptures, these words are attributed to God, Exalted is He: 'My servant who is truly My servant is he who does not wait for the cock to crow before he gets up.'

6
Invoking Blessings upon God's Messenger

The merit of invoking blessings upon God's Messenger, God bless him and give him peace; his special virtue, God bless him and give him peace

God, Exalted is He, said:

> 'God and His angels bless the Prophet. O you who believe, bless him also, and greet him with peace.' [al- Aḥzāb, 33:56]
>
> (Inna-llāha wa-malā'ikatahu yuṣallūna 'alā-lnabīyi yā ayyuhā-lladhīna āmanū ṣallū 'alayhi wa-sallimū taslīmā.)

According to Tradition: 'The Prophet, on him be peace, came one day – his face aglow with good tidings – and said: "Gabriel, on him be peace, came to me and said: 'It will surely please you to know, Muhammad, that no member of your Community ever invokes a single blessing on you without my invoking ten upon him, and that no member of your Community ever salutes you with peace without my saluting him ten times.'"'[1]

The Prophet, on him be peace, also said: 'When anyone blesses me, the angels invoke the same blessings on him; so let him give and receive accordingly, whether little or much.'[2] Said he, on him be peace: 'The person most worthy of me is he who blesses me most often.'[3]

The Messenger, on him be peace, said: 'It is the height of meanness in a believer for him to hear me mentioned and not to bless me.'[4] He said, on him be peace: 'Multiply benediction upon me on the day of Congregational Prayer (Friday).[5]

The Prophet, on him be peace, said: 'Ten good deeds are recorded in favour of any member of my Community who blesses me, and ten bad deeds are erased from his record.'[6] And he said, on him be peace: 'If anyone says, when he hears the Call to Prayer and the Signal to begin Prayer: "O God, Lord of this Perfect Call and steadfast Prayer, bless Muhammad, Your servant and Your messenger; grant him mediation, merit, exalted rank and intercession on the Day of Resurrection" – he is entitled to my intercession.'[7]

God's Messenger, on him be peace, said: 'If anyone blesses me in writing, the angels will not cease asking forgiveness for him as long as my name is in that book.'[8] He said, on him be peace: 'There are angels on earth who travel around to bring me salutation from my Community.'[9] And he said, on him be peace: 'No-one salutes me without God's restoring my spirit to me so that I may return his salutation.'[10]

When they asked him: 'O Messenger of God, how should we invoke blessings upon you?' he replied: 'Say: "O God, bless Muhammad, Your servant, and his family and his wives and his offspring, as You have blessed Abraham and the family of Abraham. Bestow Your grace upon Muhammad, his wives and his offspring, as you have bestowed Your grace upon Abraham and the family of Abraham. You are indeed Praiseworthy and Glorious."'[11]

It is related that, after the death of God's Messenger, on him be peace, 'Umar ibn al-Khaṭṭāb, may God be pleased with him, was heard weeping and saying:

'You are more to me than my father and mother, O Messenger of God! There was once a palm tree stump on which you used to stand when you addressed the people. But when the people grew in number, you adopted a pulpit to let them all hear you. The tree stump then mourned your separation, until you laid your hand upon it and it was reassured. Still greater right has your Community to pine for you now you have parted from them.

'You are more to me than my father and mother, O Messenger of God! So great is your merit in His sight that He has equated obedience to you with obedience to Himself, for He said, Great and Glorious is He: "Whoever obeys the Messenger obeys God." [al-Nisā', 4:80]

'You are more to me than my father and mother, O Messenger of God! So great is your merit in His sight that He told you you were pardoned before He told you the offence, for He said, Great and Glorious is He: "God has pardoned you – why did you grant them leave (of absence from military duty)?"* [al-Tawbah, 9:43]

'You are more to me than my father and mother, O Messenger of God! So great is your merit in His sight that He sent you as the last of the Prophets, yet mentioned you among the first of them, for He said, Great and Glorious is He: "Then We exacted a covenant from the Prophets – from you, from Noah, from Abraham . . ." [al-Aḥzāb, 33:7]

'You are more to me than my father and mother, O Messenger of God! So great is your merit in His sight that the people of Hell dearly wish they had obeyed you; as they suffer torment among its layers they say: "If only we had obeyed God, and had obeyed the Messenger!" [al-Aḥzāb, 33:66]

'You are more to me than my father and mother, O Messenger of God! While God gave Moses, son of 'Imrān, a rock from which streams gushed forth, this is not more miraculous than when water welled from your fingers, God bless you.[12]

'You are more to me than my father and mother, O Messenger of God! It is true that God gave Solomon, son of David, "the wind whose morning course was a month's journey and its evening course a month's journey." [Sabā', 34:12] Yet this was not so miraculous as Burāq, on which you ascended to the seventh heaven, then ended your night by performing the morning Prayer in the valley bed – God bless you.[13]

'You are more to me than my father and mother, O Messenger of God! God did indeed grant Jesus, Mary's son, the power to bring the dead to life. Yet this is no greater miracle than when the poisoned sheep spoke to you, roasted as it was; for its leg said to you: "Do not eat me! I am poisoned."[14]

'You are more to me than my father and mother, O Messenger of God! Noah once cursed his people, saying: "Lord, leave none of the unbelievers on the earth!" [Nūḥ,

---

* Before an important expedition in defence of Islām, the Prophet, on him be peace, had readily accepted excuses from those who did not wish to participate, without establishing whether the excuses were genuine. (Tr.)

71:26] Had you cursed us like that, we should have perished. Yet, though your back was trampled, your face bloodied and your teeth broken,[15] you refused to say anything but good; your words were: "O God, forgive my people, for they do not know."[16]

'You are more to me than my father and mother, O Messenger of God! Though your years were few and your life-span short, you were followed by many more than followed Noah, for all his great age and longevity. Many believed in you, but only a few believed along with him.

'You are more to me than my father and mother, O Messenger of God! If you had sat with none but your peer, you would not have sat with us; if you had married only your equal, you would not have trusted us. And yet, by God, you did sit with us, marry among us and trust us. You dressed in wool;[17] you rode the donkey and I rode behind you;[18] you set your food on the ground;[19] you licked your fingers in all humility[20] – God bless you and give you peace.'

Someone said: 'I used to write down Tradition, invoking blessings upon the Prophet, God bless him and give him peace, but not saluting him with peace. Then I saw the Prophet, God bless him and give him peace, in a dream, in which he said to me: "Do you not complete the benediction for me in your writing?" Since then I have never written without invoking upon him both blessings and peace.'

Abūl Ḥasan is reported as saying: 'I saw the Prophet, on him be peace, in a dream, and I said: "O Messenger of God, with what was al-Shāfi'ī rewarded on your behalf, for saying in his book, *al-Risāla*: 'And God bless Muhammad – as the mindful remember and the heedless forget to mention'?" Said he, God bless him and give him peace: "He was rewarded on my behalf with not having to face the Reckoning."'

7
The Merit of Seeking Forgiveness

ISTIGHFĀR

God, Great and Glorious is He, says: 'Those who, when they have committed an indecency or wronged themselves, remember God and seek forgiveness for their sins . . .' [Āl 'Imrān, 3:135]

According to 'Alqama and al-Aswad, 'Abdullāh ibn Mas'ūd said: 'In the Book of God, Great and Glorious is He, there are two Verses. If a servant recites them after committing a sin, and if he seeks God's forgiveness, God will forgive him. They are:

> "Those who, when they have committed an indecency or wronged themselves . . ." [Āl Imrān, 3:135]
>
> (Wa-lladhīna idhā fa'alū fāḥishatan aw ẓalamū anfusahum.)

and:

> "He who does evil or wrongs himself, but then seeks forgiveness of God, will find God Forgiving, Compassionate."' [al-Nisā', 4:110]
>
> (Wa-man ya'mal sū'an aw yaẓlim nafsahū thumma yastaghfiri-llāha yajidi-llāha ghafūrun raḥīmā.)

God, Great and Glorious is He, says: 'Celebrate the praises of your Lord and seek His forgiveness. Surely He is Ever-relenting.' [al-Naṣr, 110:3]

The Exalted One also says: 'Those who seek forgiveness in the early morning hours . . .' [Āl 'Imrān, 3:17]

God's Messenger, on him be peace, would often say: 'O God, to You be all glory and praise! O God, forgive me. Surely You are the Ever-relenting and Compassionate One.'[1]

Other sayings of the Prophet, on him be peace:

'To one who often seeks His forgiveness, God, Great and Glorious is He, grants relief from all troubles, a way out of all distress, and sustenance beyond his expectation.'[2]

'I seek forgiveness of God, Exalted is He, and turn to Him in repentance seventy times a day.'[3] (Even though his past and future sins had been forgiven!)

'My heart becomes clouded unless I seek forgiveness of God, Exalted is He, one hundred times a day.'[4]

'Though your sins be as many as the flecks of foam on the sea, the grains of sand in the desert, the leaves on the trees or the days of the world, God will forgive them if you say three times at bedtime: "I seek forgiveness of the One Almighty God, the Ever-living, the Self-subsisting, and I repent to Him."'[5] (According to another Tradition, this will obtain forgiveness 'even for one who deserts the ranks.')[6]

Ḥudhayfa said: 'I used to speak harshly to my family, so I said to God's Messenger, on him be peace: "O Messenger of God, I fear that my tongue may lead me to Hell." The blessed Prophet replied: "How about seeking forgiveness? I beg God's forgiveness a hundred times each day."'

'Ā'isha, may God be pleased with her, said: 'God's Messenger, on him be peace, said to me: "If you have committed a sin, seek forgiveness of God and repent to Him. Repentance of sin means feeling remorse and seeking forgiveness."'

God's Messenger, on him be peace, used to seek forgiveness with this Prayer: 'O God, forgive me my mistakes, my ignorance, my extravagance and what You know better than I. O God, forgive me my frivolity and my over-earnestness, my faults and wrong intentions and all my shortcomings. O God, forgive me what I have done in the past and what I shall do in the future, what I have done in secret and what I have done in public, and what You know better than I. You are the Advancer and the Delayer and over all things You have power.'[7]

'Alī, may God be pleased with him, said: 'I am the sort of man who would benefit as much as God allowed from hearing a Tradition from God's Messenger, on him be peace. When one of his Companions told me a Tradition, I would ask him to swear to its authenticity. I would trust him once he had sworn. Abū Bakr, may God be pleased with him, was always truthful. He once told me he had heard God's Messenger, on him be peace, say: "If someone commits a sin, but then takes a thorough ritual ablution, performs a Prayer of two cycles and seeks forgiveness of God, Great and Glorious is He, his sin will be forgiven." Then Abū Bakr recited the Verse: "Those who, when they have committed an indecency or wronged themselves . . ."' [Āl 'Imrān, 3:135]

According to Abū Hurayra, may God be pleased with him, the Prophet, on him be peace, said: 'When a believer commits a sin, a black spot forms on his heart. If he repents and mends his ways and seeks forgiveness, the spot is purged from his heart. But if he goes on sinning, the spot will grow until it covers his heart all over.' That is the 'rust' which God, Great and Glorious is He, mentions in His Book:

> 'No indeed! What they have earned is rust on their hearts.' [al-Muṭaffifīn, 83:14]
>
> (Kallā bal rāna 'alā qulūbihim mā kānū yaksibūn.)

According to Abū Hurayra, may God be pleased with him, the Prophet, on him be peace, said: 'God, Glorified and Exalted is He, will raise His servant to high rank in Paradise and he will say: "My Lord, how have I deserved this?" Then God, Great and Glorious is He, will say: "By virtue of your son's Prayer for forgiveness on your behalf."'[8]

According to 'Ā'isha, may God be pleased with her, God's Messenger, on him be peace, said: 'O God, make me one of those who rejoice when they have done a good deed, and who seek forgiveness when they have done something bad.'[9]

God's Messenger, on him be peace, said: 'When a man commits a sin and says: "O God, forgive me!" God, Great and Glorious is He, says: "My servant has committed a sin, but he knows he has a Lord who takes account of sin and forgives it. O My servant, do what you want, for I have already forgiven you."'[10]

Other sayings of the Prophet, on him be peace:

'A man who seeks forgiveness is not a persistent sinner, even if he lapses seventy times a day.'[11]

'A man who has never done a good deed looks heavenwards and says: "Surely I have a Lord. O Lord, forgive me!" and God, Great and Glorious is He, says: "I have already forgiven you."'[12]

'If a man commits a sin, but knows that God sees him, he will receive forgiveness even without asking for it.'[13]

'God, Exalted is He, says: "O My servants, you are all sinners except for those I have pardoned. So seek My forgiveness and I will forgive you. I will gladly forgive anyone who knows that I possess the power to forgive him."'[14]

'If a man says: "Glory be to You! I have wronged myself and done something bad, so forgive me, for there is no one to forgive sins but You," his sins are forgiven, even if they are like a trail of ants.'[15]

It is related that the best Prayer for forgiveness is this: 'O God, You are my Lord and I am Your servant. You created me. I am fulfilling my covenant and promise to You as best I can. I take refuge with You from the evil I have perpetrated. I acknowledge You as the source of my blessings, and I acknowledge my own responsibility for my sins. I have wronged myself and I confess my sin, so forgive me my sins – those I have committed in the past and those I shall commit in future. Surely no one forgives all sins but You.'[16]

Other wise sayings:

Khālid ibn Ma'dan said: 'God, Great and Glorious is He, says: "Dearest to Me of My servants are those who love one another for love of Me, whose hearts are bound to the Mosque, and who seek forgiveness at the break of day. When I wish to punish the rest of earth's people, I shall remember them; I shall leave them alone and turn the punishment away from them."'

Qatāda said: 'The Quran shows you your sickness and your medicine. Your sickness is sin and your medicine is the Prayer for forgiveness.'

'Alī, may God ennoble his countenance, said: 'It puzzles me that a man should perish when he possesses the means to save himself.' When they asked him to explain, he said: 'The Prayer for forgiveness!'

He also used to say: 'God, Glorified and Exalted is he, never inspires a man to seek forgiveness if He intends to punish him.'

Al-Fuḍayl said: 'When a servant says: "I seek God's forgiveness," the meaning of his words is: "Let my sins be few!"'

A certain scholar said: 'Man is between sin and grace. Nothing can improve matters except praising God and seeking His forgiveness.'

Al-Rabī' ibn Khaytham said: 'Beware of saying: "I seek God's forgiveness and I repent to Him," for it is a sin and a lie if not acted upon. It is better to say: "O God, forgive me and turn towards me."'

Al-Fuḍayl said: 'To seek forgiveness without renunciation is the repentance of liars.'

Rābi'a al-'Adawīya, may God be pleased with her, said: 'Our Prayer for forgiveness needs many Prayers for forgiveness.'

A wise man said: 'To seek forgiveness without feeling remorse is to mock God, Great and Glorious is He, without being aware of it.'

A Bedouin was heard to say, as he clung to the covering of the Ka'ba: 'O God, I seek Your forgiveness, although I shamefully persist in sin. How could I stop begging Your forgiveness, when I know how generously You pardon? What loving kindness You bestow on me, when You have no need of me at all! How often I offend and anger You, although I need You so badly! What a Lord – He fulfils all His promises, yet pardons when he threatens! Take my great sin into Your mighty pardon, O Most Compassionate of the compassionate!'

Abū 'Abdullāh al-Warrāq said: 'Though your sins be as numerous as raindrops and the flecks of foam on the sea, they will be wiped away from you, God willing, if you offer this supplication to your Lord in all sincerity: "O God, I beg Your forgiveness for every sin, for I have lapsed again after turning to You in repentance. I seek Your forgiveness for all the promises I have made to You, but failed to carry out. I ask Your forgiveness for every action I intended to do for Your sake alone, but that I mixed with something other than You. I seek Your forgiveness for every blessing You have bestowed on me, but that I used in disobedience of You. O Knower of the invisible and of the visible, I beg Your forgiveness for every sin I have committed by the light of day and in the darkness of night, in public and in solitude, in secret and for all to see. O Benevolent One!"' Some say this is the Prayer for forgiveness used by the Prophet Adam, on him be peace. According to others, it is the supplication of the Prophet Khiḍr, on him be peace.

Abbreviations used in Notes to Traditions cited:

AD	– Abā Dā'ūd
Aḥ	– Aḥmad
B	– al-Bukhārī
Baz	– al-Bazzār
Bhq	– al-Baihaqī
Drq	– al-Dāraquṭnī
Ḥkm	– al-Ḥākim
Ḥrth	– al-Ḥārith
Ḥsn b. Sa'īd	– Ḥasan ibn Sa'īd
IḤib	– Ibn Ḥibbān
IM	– Ibn Māja
'Ir	– al-'Irāqī
M	– Muslim
Mbrk	– Ibn al-Mubārak
Nas	– al-Nasā'ī
Ṭbr	– al-Ṭabarānī
frm	– al-Tirmidhī

Notes

Chapter 1: The Prayer

1 Trm: ḥasan.
2 B.
3 Ṭbr/Ḥsn b. Sa'īd: ḍa'īf.
4 B/M.
5 AD/Nas/IM et al.
6 M.
7 M.
8 Mālik: mursal.
9 Ṭbr – different wording.
10 Bhq et al: ḍa'īf.
11 B/M.
12 Aḥmad.
13 AD.
14 Ṭbr – latter part only.
15 Baz – doubtful isnād.
16 Aḥ/Bhq.
17 Ḥkm.
18 Untraced.
19 Bhq – uncertain isnād.
20 Mbrk – mursal.
21 Ḥrth: spurious acc. 'Ir.
22 Aḥ–ṣaḥīḥ.
23 Ibn 'Adī.
24 Ṭbr/Bhq – ḍa'īf.
25 B/M.
26 B/M.
27 M.
28 Not traced beyond Sa'īd ibn al-Musayyab.
29 Trm.
30 Mbrk – mursal.
31 IM/M.
32 M.
33 M.
34 M/IM/Aḥ.
35 B/M – slightly different version.
36 Trm/Nas.
37 AD/Trm: ḥasan-ṣaḥīḥ.
38 IM/Ḥkm/Bhq.
39 Ṭbr – ṣaḥīḥ (slight variant.)
40 Azdī – mursal.
41 Untraced in this wording.
42 Trm – ḍa'īf.
43 IM – ṣaḥīḥ; also B/M – without comparison to grouse's nest.
44 Ṭbr – ḍa'īf.
45 B/M.
46 Drq – ḍa'īf.
47 B/M.
48 IḤib/Ḥkm.
49 Abū Na'īm – ḍa'īf. Variant with sound isnād goes back to the Companions.
50 IM/Ḥkm – ṣaḥīḥ.
51 Emphatic particle *innamā,* followed by the definite article *al-.*
52 Nas.
53 Ad/Nas.
54 B/M.
55 'Welfare due': see p. 53.

56 Ad/Nas.
57 AD (from 'Uthmān ibn Ṭalḥa, not 'Uthmān ibn Abī Shayba).
58 B/M.
59 Mbrk.
60 Abū 'Abdullāh ibn Ḥaqīq.
61 Nas.
62 Mālik.
63 Untraced.
64 Ah – ṣaḥīḥ.
65 Untraced.
66 Nas – ṣaḥīḥ (abridged version).

Chapter 2: Almsgiving

1 AD/Trm/Ḥkm from Ibn 'Umar (except last sentence).
2 E.g. al-Nakha'ī, al-Sha'bī, 'Aṭā' and Mujāhid.
3 al-Manāwī.
4 B/M.
5 Aḥmad et al.
6 Abū Nu'aym: ḍa'īf.
7 al-Khaṭīb: ḍa'īf.
8 B/M.
9 Trm: ḥasan.
10 Untraced in this formulation.
11 Ibn 'Adī and Ibn Ḥibbān: ḍa'īf.
12 Untraced.
13 Bhq: ḍa'īf.
14 B/M.
15 Not marfū'.
16 Untraced.
17 Ibn 'Adī and Bazzār.
18 Nas/IḤib: ṣaḥīḥ.
19 AD/Trm.
20 Ibn al-Mubārak.
21 Idem.
22 Elements of this Tradition have been traced through al-Baihaqī and Ibn Ḥibbān.
23 Aḥmad/Ṭbr: ḍa'īf.
24 Many slight variants: AD/B/M et al.
25 AD reports a Tradition of similar import.

Chapter 3: Fasting

1 Ḥkm: ṣaḥīḥ.
2 Azdī (from Jābān, not Jābir): ḍa'īf.
3 As reported by Bishr ibn Ḥārith.
4 B/M.
5 Aḥmad: majhūl.
6 Ṭbr: ḍa'īf.
7 Nas/IM.
8 Kharā'iṭī: ḥasan.
9 AD.
10 See p. 76.

Chapter 4: The Pilgrimage

1 Trm: gharīb.
2 al-Bukhārī and Muslim.
3 Mālik: mursal.
4 Unknown to al-'Irāqī.
5 Baihaqī/Dāraquṭnī: ḍa'īf.
6 B/M.
7 Ibn Māja.
8 Khaṭīb.
9 Bhq: ḥasan.
10 Ḥākim: ṣaḥīḥ.
11 Trm: ḥasan.
12 B/M.
13 Hkm: ṣaḥīḥ.
14 Unidentified.
15 Trm/Nasā'ī: ṣaḥīḥ.
16 B/M.
17 Ḥkm: ṣaḥīḥ.
18 B/M.
19 Trm: ḥasan.
20 Azraqī: mawqūf.

21 Bazzār et al.: ṣaḥīḥ.
22 Unidentified.
23 Trm et al.: ṣaḥīḥ.
24 B/M.
25 Untraced in this wording; authenticated variants in Ibn Māja.
26 Abū Hurayra, Ibn 'Umar, Abū Sa'īd.
27 Trm: ḥasan-ṣaḥīḥ.
28 B/M.
29 Aḥmad/al-Ṭabarānī.
30 Khaṭīb/Ṣābūnī (with slight variations).
31 Bhq: ḍa'īf.
32 Ibn 'Adī from Mu'ādh.
33 Aḥmad: layyin/Ḥkm (shorter version): ṣaḥīḥ.
34 Trm/IM.
35 Ḥkm.
36 M/Nas.
37 Baghawī/Ṭbr.
38 Also Aḥmad (variant).
39 Trm/IM: gharīb.
40 Ḥkm/Aḥmad.
41 Abū Dā'ūd.
42 Aḥ/Ḥkm.
43 Ṭbr.
44 AD.
45 Trm/IM et al.
46 Trm.
47 IM/Bhq.
48 Untraced.
49 Many variant wordings: AD/Bhq/Trm/Nas/IM et al.
50 Bhq.
51 Baz/Drq.
52 AD: ṣaḥīḥ.
53 'Abdullah ibn 'Umar.
54 Possibly referring to a weak Tradition from Fāṭima, may God be pleased with her.
55 B/M with very slightly different wording.
56 Nas et al.
57 M.

Chapter 5: The Night Vigil

1 B/M.
2 B/M.
3 Ṭbr/Baz.
4 Ibn Abī Iyās et al.: mursal.
5 Saḥiḥ.
6 B/M.
7 al-'Irāqī does not consider this Tradition authentic.
8 Ṭbr/Bhq: ḥasan.
9 Nas/IM: ṣaḥiḥ.
10 Ibn Abīl Dunyā: mursal.
11 Untraced.
12 B/M (without mention of Gabriel, on him be peace).
13 IḤib.
14 AD/IM.
15 AD/IM.
16 Ad/Nas: ṣaḥīḥ.
17 M.
18 M.

Chapter 6: Invoking Blessings upon God's Messenger

1 Nas et al.
2 IM/Ṭbr.
3 Trm.
4 Trm et al.
5 5 AD et al.
6 'Amr ibn Dīnār.
7 (Variant.)
8 Ṭbr: ḍa'īf.
9 Nas et al.
10 AD.
11 B/M.
12 B/M.
13 B/M (part).
14 AD: munqaṭi'.
15 B/M.
16 Bhq.
17 al-Ṭayālisī.
18 B/M.
19 Aḥmad.
20 M.

Chapter 7: The Merit of Seeking Forgiveness

1 Ḥkm.
2 AD/Nas.
3 B.
4 M.
5 Trm.
6 AD/Trm.
7 B/M.
8 Aḥmad.
9 Aḥmad.
10 B/M.
11 Trm: gharīb.
12 Untraced.
13 Ṭbr.
14 Trm: ḥasan.
15 Bhq.
16 B/Nas (many slight variations transmitted).